MANGOES ON THE MOON

June 2006.

By the same author:

Seeds of Trouble: Government Policy and Land Rights in Nyasaland, 1946-1964
Development Governor: A Biography of Sir Geoffrey Colby
State of Emergency: Crisis in Central Africa, Nyasaland 1959-1960
Retreat From Empire: Sir Robert Armitage in Africa and Cyprus
Sir Glyn Jones*: A Proconsul in Africa*
Revolt of the Ministers: The Malawi Cabinet Crisis
Wild Goose: the Life and Death of Hugh van Oppen
A Fine Chest of Medals: the Life of Jack Archer
Chipembere: the Missing Years
Johnston's Administration: A History of the British Central Africa Administration, 1891-1897
The Evolution of Local Government in Malawi
Education and Research in Public Administration in Africa (with A. Adedeji)
Ife Essays in Public Administration (with M. J. Balogun)

MANGOES ON THE MOON:

A NYASALAND-MALAWI ANTHOLOGY OF ANECDOTES

Anecdote: a narrative of an amusing or striking incident, originally an item of gossip.
Anecdotes: secret or hitherto unpublished details of history.
Oxford English Dictionary.

The purpose is to inform and entertain.
BBC Charter.

COLIN BAKER

Mpemba Books
Cardiff

Published in 2006
by Mpemba Books

ISBN 0-9542020-2-3

Photoset in 10 Times New Roman by Mpemba Books, Cardiff
Printed and bound by Cromwell Press, Trowbridge

For my family:
Shirley, Christopher, Daryll, Catherine, Lynette,
Martin, Charlotte, William and Edward.

PREFACE

There was things that he stretched, but mainly he told the truth.
Mark Twain, 'The Adventures of Huckleberry Finn'.

As I was writing one of the pieces in this anthology I was asked by a close friend whose judgement and advice I have always valued most highly, 'Did that really happen?' I found this question disconcerting because although the answer could truthfully have been 'Yes', fuller truthfulness would have required me to add 'But not quite like that.' And that sent my mind back to three events.

One event occurred while I was at school and having lunch one day. I have long forgotten the subject of conversation but I do recall that one of the prefects at table used the expression, 'That's very true.' The headmaster, who was lunching with the prefects, gave it as his opinion that one could not validly use the term 'very true'. 'Either a thing is true or it is not true, in which latter case it is false. There are no degrees of truth.' He spoke kindly and since he was a Doctor of Philosophy I guess we all accepted his view without thinking too much about it. At least I did not think much about it until many years later when my mind again reflected on truthfulness.

This time it was in 1969, on the day the Americans first landed on the moon. It was evening and I was standing on the lawn with our cook, Sanudi, outside the house in which we were then living. The air was still, the moon was full – it looked fuller than usual – and we were both admiring it. The news of the landing had only just been announced on the radio and as we looked up I pointed to the moon and commented on the way in which men were, at that very moment, wandering about its surface. As I pointed upwards I glanced sideways at my companion and found that he was not looking at the moon but at me. I repeated the news and he simply said, 'Yes, of course, *Bwana*.' What I was saying was fact, what he was hearing was fiction.

The third memory stirred by my friend's recent question, 'Did that really happen?' was some twenty years later. I was writing about the Devlin Commission which looked into the factors leading to the 1959 state of emergency declared that year in Nyasaland. I was concerned about a number of aspects of Sir Patrick Devlin's conduct of the inquiry and puzzled by his repeated statement that his job was to 'get at the truth'. What most concerned me was the way in which he, and English judges generally, used a very limited range of measurements to 'get at the truth' and decide whether or not something 'really happened'. Judges require either satisfaction beyond reasonable doubt in a criminal case, or satisfaction on the balance of probabilities in a civil action. They have to decide one way or the other; they cannot say, as others might, 'I'm damned if I know.' It seemed to me that Devlin had available to him a very much wider range than these two possibilities, reasonable doubt and balance of probabilities. The range extends from incontrovertible conviction - Gilbert's 'no manner of doubt, no probable, possible manner of doubt, no possible doubt whatever' - through nearly certain, highly probable, probable, just possible, improbable and highly improbable to utterly impossible – 'Come off it, mate' - and there are many gradations in between. Aristotle preferred probable impossibilities to improbable possibilities, and James Callaghan declared during the July 1959 House of Commons debate on the Nyasaland emergency, 'If you believe that, you'll believe anything.' It is a sliding scale, not a scale with only two balancing points.

I wondered, too, about painters, sculptors and musicians and how they presented their subject matter. Is Annigoni's portrait of Queen Elizabeth II more real or more truthful than, say, Sutherland's? Is Michelangelo's David more truthful than Epstein's? And what about the storm in Beethoven's sixth symphony when set beside that in Verdi's Rigoletto? We may prefer the work of one of them more - sometimes much more - than that of the other, but is one of these painters, one of these sculptors and one of these composers more truthful than the other? And if some of the ancient Greek philosophers considered poetry to be more worthy of serious attention than history, what of the historical poem?

In relating these thoughts to the anecdotes in this anthology, although I know that some are closer to the truth end of the truth-false spectrum - or closer to the fact end of the fact-fiction scale - than are others, how will other people know? And does it matter if they are unsure or mistaken? I toyed with the idea that in some cases I ought to end the anecdote with the words 'or so 'tis said', but there might be so many of these that it would become tedious. Eventually, relying on the efficacy of the moral teaching given to readers at their mother's knee and on their ability to distinguish truth from falsehood and fact from fiction, I decided to give a minimum of guidance. The guidance is this: except for the limericks - which in most, but not all, cases are pure fiction - there is truth in each of the anecdotes, though some teeter nervously at the extreme fiction end of the spectrum while others sit smugly on the outermost limit of the other end.

In the afternoon of 26 January 1788, eleven ships of the First Fleet dropped anchor at Sydney Cove, in south-east Australia, with soldiers and prisoners setting out to establish a settlement for British convicts. Today Sydney is a large cosmopolitan city and its Cove has grown into a bustling harbour, edged by a broad horseshoe shaped promenade known as the Circular Quay. Here office workers jog or walk briskly at lunch time; buskers, musicians, jugglers and acrobats entertain the crowds; visitors sip coffee, dunk biscuits, lick ice creams and watch the ferry boats entering and leaving the harbour in quick succession, or simply sit on benches enjoying the sun. Embedded in the broad pavement of the promenade is a circular bronze plaque. It commemorates the visit in 1895 - half way between the First Fleet's arrival and the present day - of the remarkable American writer, Mark Twain, who was undertaking a round the world lecture tour. In

Australia he was told of the country's history and, as is the case today with visitors to their land, his Australian hosts recounted the past in terms of local stories about how various events happened. Twain was fascinated, and when shortly he wrote about his visit, he said of Australian history, 'It does not read like history. It reads more like the most beautiful lies.' It would be comforting, if somewhat fanciful, to think that, faced with the Nyasaland-Malawi anecdotes in this anthology, Twain might, in his generosity, say the same of those that seem to fall short of that complete truth which my headmaster believed to be the only truth and to which my friend hoped I would aspire, if not in practice adhere.

CONTENTS

THE NCHIMA TRUST

The Nchima Trust is a small, very active and much admired charity, originally founded in 1962 by the Gardiner family. Its early operations were in the Thyolo and Blantyre Districts in the Southern Region of Malawi. Later, the Trust extended its activities to meet the needs of individuals and communities throughout the country. The Trust provides funds only for projects within Malawi. Donations are presently concentrated on Health, Education, Rural Credit, Orphan Support and a thriving Community Centre at Thyolo. Where the need arises, and when funds permit, the Trustees may choose to support any project which, to them, seems appropriate.

The author wrote this Anthology of Nyasaland-Malawi Anecdotes as a gift to the Nchima Trust, and at his request all proceeds from its sale will go to the Trust to further their excellent work in the Warm Heart of Africa.

PAULOS

I first met Paulos when I was Assistant District Commissioner in the Southern Province of Nyasaland and he was a chief's messenger. Short and stocky of build, with twinkling eyes in a laughing face across the breadth of which stretched the widest nose I have ever seen, he enjoyed, as he put it, 'catching bad men'.

Every so often he would come to me, usually in a secluded spot as dusk was falling so that our conversation should not be overheard by others, and he would confidentially whisper in my ear that he knew where there were some 'bad men' – usually tax defaulters. Would I like him to 'catch 'em' for me? If I asked for further details about these bad men and their whereabouts, he would shift from one bare and dust covered foot to the other and indicate that a man in my exalted position need not bother himself with such details. Eventually I learned not to ask. Usually I would say that it would be very kind and public spirited of him if he were to catch these bad men of whom he spoke, but that he must do so lawfully. On hearing this he would look at me with a pained and disappointed expression as if to say, 'How could you possibly think that I, Paulos, could ever do anything unlawful? Here I am, offering to deploy my skills in helping the Government, and you appear to think that I might not act within the law. Have you forgotten that I am a chief's messenger with ample authority to catch bad men under what you district officers call native law and custom?' His facial expression was quite sufficient to encompass and convey such thoughts without his speaking a word. Paulos would then turn to begin his bad men catching mission, would hesitate, and add, 'This may be a dangerous operation and since I shall not be in uniform I need some symbol of authority.' In the early days I asked what he had in mind and he invariably answered, 'Handcuffs, *Bwana*.' These I provided and off he went.

Although he would often be gone for several weeks at a time, without fail he would return with at least one handcuffed 'bad man', or if there were two they would be handcuffed together. They invariably pleaded guilty at their subsequent and hastily convened court hearing and, since Paulos always testified that they 'had come quietly', they received a light sentence of a month or so penal labour, for which public work they were paid a small sum as *posho*. In this way they were fed at the Government's expense in exchange for mild labour repairing roads, under – and this will not surprise you – the gentle supervision of Paulos.

At the end of their sentence Paulos would disappear for a few weeks and then emerge to arrange another dusk time tryst. Again he would offer his specialist services to 'catch a bad man' and, pleased with his last performance, I would agree. It was only when he asked for another 'symbol of authority' that I recalled that he had not returned the last pair of handcuffs that I had given him. He had a variety of explanations, usually indicating that he had lost them in a dangerous scuffle when trying to 'catch' other 'bad men'. For reasons long since forgotten, there seemed to be an ample supply of handcuffs in the *boma* store for which I was never asked to account. Indeed, had I been asked to account for any of them I would have claimed that they had disappeared in the course of a scuffle involving 'catching bad men' and that I would call Paulos to corroborate this.

In due course, I was posted to the Central Province. I had not long been there when the head clerk said that a strange man was insisting on seeing me but was refusing to give any indication of his business. Indeed, he made it clear that a serious fate would await the head clerk if I knew that he was being barred from immediate entry. Puzzled, I asked for him to be shown in. There was no mistaking the broadly ginning face and uniquely broad nose that appeared round the door: Paulos. We had a great chat, exchanged family news and told each other how we had been getting on. I asked what brought him the long distance to the Central Province, and at this point he glanced furtively round to ensure that the door was securely shut and no one was listening at the windows. Leaning close to me, in a hushed voice he whispered that he had learned, to his great consternation, that there were some 'bad men' in the District and, pausing while he studied my face and reaction, asked if I would like him to 'catch 'em' for me. How could I refuse, he silently enquired. After all, his past performance clearly indicated a one hundred per cent catch rate, he had travelled long distances to assist me and the Government, and he knew positively that my reputation for tax collection and the apprehension of tax defaulters and other malefactors in the South had been much admired by no less a person than the Governor himself. Would I not be a fool to pass up the opportunity to establish a similar reputation in the Central Province? On this and several subsequent occasions I accepted Paulos's offer - always at the cost of yet another pair of handcuffs.

Eventually, I was posted to a different District in the Central Province, this time as District Commissioner. With the pressure of work and my new responsibilities, Paulos passed from my mind, partly because I was able to delegate the major portion of tax collecting work to the Assistant District Commissioner. Then came the day when the head clerk came to tell me that there was an unusual man outside demanding, without explanation, to see me immediately. I enquired no further and simply said, with happy anticipation, 'Show him in, please, and shut the door.' Paulos! With lowered voice, he revealed that, excellent as the administration of the District undoubtedly was under my charge, I would no doubt be astonished to learn that there were, lurking in un-revealed corners of the District, a number of 'bad men' who, in the absence of being 'caught' would, he feared, tarnish my reputation as a DC and cause alarm and despondency throughout the District. Would I like him …? After a quick check to see that there was an adequate supply of handcuffs in the *boma* store, Paulos was in business again.

My final posting in Nyasaland, by this time Malawi, was to an office job, where my duties were not those of a DC and where I had no responsibility for tax collection and the apprehension of evil doers. What I had overlooked was that my office was close to the area where Paulos lived and where I had first met him many years previously. Had I not overlooked this I would inevitably have expected him to pitch up at my office as dusk fell one evening - as indeed he did. I think he must have anticipated my response: that although I was delighted to see him, there were, unfortunately, no circumstances in which I could possibly require his services in 'catching bad men'. A look of uncomprehending disappointment and sadness crossed his face. Not sadness and disappointment over the absence of the need to employ his skills, but over my failure to see the obvious even though it was under my nose. He could understand this if my nose enjoyed the view blocking dimensions of his own but, unfortunately for me in his opinion, it did not. The dangers presented by 'bad men' in the past were nothing when compared with those in which I now found myself. A long serving and successful Administrative Officer, such as I had become, inevitably accumulated many possessions of remarkable value in his home which – and he knew this for a fact – had already attracted the attention of 'bad men' locally and from as far afield as the mining compounds of South Africa. What I needed was a watchman to guard my home – and protect my young children, with whom over the years he had become a great favourite – and keep 'bad men' at bay. If I was concerned that I no longer had access to a supply of handcuffs, I need not worry, for he had his own pair; indeed he had several pairs! Thus, Paulos became the watchman at my house and, as he put it, my personal bodyguard.

When the time came for me and my family to leave Malawi, Paulos was the final person to whom we said goodbye. By this time we had known each other for many years. Our relationship had brought pleasure, admiration and a degree of amusement to me and a certain status to him, for no one was ever told just what we discussed in secluded spots as dusk fell – maybe Paulos was a Special Branch officer in disguise, maybe even in the pay of MI5 or the CIA, or was bringing me clandestine messages from the Governor. We were both sad at the parting. Yet our last words were not about this. To my surprise, he looked at me with a grin and muttered two words: 'Ten Shillings.' He saw that I was puzzled and he explained, 'I thought you were going to ask for how much I sold the handcuffs. It was ten shillings a pair – more or less – but there were lots of them!'

THE MAP

On one of the walls in the office of the Provincial Commissioner in Blantyre there was a large and splendidly drawn map that stretched from the red polished concrete floor to the white-washed reed matting ceiling, marking the various types of land-holding in the Southern Province. Trust land was coloured red, private land was coloured blue and leasehold land was coloured green. There was, however, an intriguing, large, irregular shaped area in the south-eastern corner of the map which was tinted a rather fetching pale shade of lime-yellow. No such colour appeared on the legend to the map. When asked about this area, the Provincial Commissioner rather haughtily replied, 'Oh, that. That's where my Secretary's damned dog peed on it.'

ooo ☺ ☻ ooo

IN VINO VERITAS

And Noah he often said to his wife when they sat down to dine,
'I don't mind where the water goes if it doesn't get into the wine.'
G K Chesterton.

I

We had been invited to lunch at the home of the French ambassador and his wife. The ambassador was a quiet and somewhat introverted man, who regrettably and quite unjustifiably did not universally command the respect of his staff. The cultural attaché, a somewhat pompous graduate of the Sorbonne, for example, claimed that His Excellency was not suited to diplomatic life, having spent much of his career as 'a mechanic on an oil tanker' though in fact he had been captain of several large battleships of the French fleet. His wife, on the other hand, was a popular, vivacious, very attractive, entertaining and lively hostess.

Among the other guests was a grey bearded, dignified French priest, a humble man of great learning, dressed in his usual white cassock – much cleaner on this occasion than on others when working in the bush – and he was seated next to the ambassador's wife. The conversation at this end of the table was cultured and learned, a mixture of good humoured badinage and philosophical musings, and conducted, in both French and English, in elegant tones. The priest and the ambassador's wife were clearly enjoying it. The conversation turned to wines and the ambassador's wife teasingly asked the priest's opinion of that most recently served at table, a pale white wine of manifestly exceptional quality, adding with a sparkle in her eye that in his profession as a rural missionary priest he no doubt had become expert in the qualities of numerous wines. Conversation elsewhere round the table stopped as the guests waited to hear the verdict of this cultured and learned man. He took a long sip from his glass, pondered thoughtfully for a moment or two and replied, with a twinkle in his eyes that matched the sparkle in those of his hostess, 'Pure angel's piss, Madame, pure angel's piss.'

II

Less diplomatic and more embarrassing language was used on a similar occasion when the Chief Justice and his wife invited us to dinner – we lived next door to them and not infrequently were invited to make up numbers at table. On this particular occasion other guests included a young magistrate and his wife and the Commissioner of Income Tax and his wife. The magistrate and I wore dinner jackets and black ties, and when the Commissioner appeared in a lounge suit the Chief Justice discreetly asked us, since we both lived nearby, if we would mind popping home and changing into lounge suits so that the Commissioner would feel less embarrassed. We did so. Shortly after our return, the Commissioner walked quietly into the drawing room and, having hastily returned to his own home, was himself now dressed in dinner jacket and black tie!

Dinner, none the less, went ahead and was a relaxed, gentle, enjoyable affair, with the guests' wine glasses frequently being replenished. Later in the evening, as a yet another bottle was being poured, the Chief Justice, temporarily forgetting that the longer the evening the poorer the quality of wine served, and forgetting that his own cellar was no doubt seriously being depleted, enquired from his end of the table to his wife at the other end, 'Barbara, is this wine off?' His wife sensibly feigned not to hear him, but he repeated the question, now more loudly, 'Barbara, is this wine off?' She once more ignored the question. Yet again her husband persisted, demanding, now almost shouting, to know, 'Barbara, is this wine off?' Eventually, unable to avoid answering her husband any longer, she looked at him sweetly and said, 'Yes, Darling, it is. Now shut up and finish your dinner!'

III

I have only once in my life sent back a bottle of wine, and, as if subconsciously to make up for this restraint, on the occasion on which I returned it, I sent back two bottles. On my father's advice, my normal way of replying to the waiter when asked to taste the wine, was to say, 'Um. Yes, though another fortnight would have made all the difference.' On this occasion, at a lakeshore hotel in Nyasaland, however, the wine was so badly clouded and gritty that I picked up sufficient courage to send it back. The second bottle was no better and indeed, if anything, was even more cloudy and gritty. I sent it back too. The third bottle was brought and as the waiter approached the table, he lifted the bottle upside-down, held it to the light, gave it a hefty shake, leaned over and whispered confidentially in my ear, 'The trouble with this place, *Bwana*, is that they keep the wine too long.'

IV

The road between Ncheu and Dedza wove its way, often through magnificent scenery, along the border between Nyasaland and Mozambique, being at various points in the former country and at various others in the latter. At only one point, however, were customs posts erected, the other crossings, for practical reasons, being ignored. Whilst the Portuguese customs officers were relaxed about their duties, those of the Nyasaland Government took them seriously and granted very few customs exemptions on goods brought in from Mozambique. By the roadside, along the border on the Mozambique side, there were a number of small general purpose stores selling such goods as sugar, soap, matches, paraffin and cloth to the local African villagers, and wine to Europeans who passed along the road travelling by car between north and south Nyasaland. The wine was cheap, of acceptable quality – though often only barely so – and sold in large glass demijohns with a basket-work covering and sealed with plaster of Paris round the cork and neck. Usually, the purchaser would later decant the wine into smaller wine bottles and seal the corks with candle wax.

Though cheap to purchase, having regard to its quality the wine became significantly less good value for money when customs duty was levied on it. To overcome this disadvantage, there had grown up over the years an elaborate means of evading the duty. The Portuguese owner of each wine-selling store employed a small team of superficially nondescript but gifted men, agile and well experienced in bush craft, whose job it was to take the demijohns when purchased, through the bush, creeping, ducking, dodging and lying low, to a point along the road beyond the Nyasaland customs post, while the purchaser drove through the post with nothing to declare and, once clear of the post and any wandering overly-vigilant customs officer, awaited the arrival of the carrier and the wine. Frequently the carrier arrived before the purchaser, despite the pickup points often being several miles beyond the customs post. It is said that the paths taken by the carriers were so well worn that they could easily be seen from aircraft flying high over the area. It is said, too, that the bush craft skills of these men subsequently made them valuable recruits to the Frelimo guerrilla army in their country's struggle for independence from Portugal. It is also said that it was the service afforded to thirsty British travellers by the loyal wine-carrying, customs-dodging, bastinado-risking, palmatoria-threatened Mozambiquan Africans over many years that Mozambique was later offered membership of the British Commonwealth.

V

From the very earliest days of mankind, wine and other forms of intoxicating liquor have been honoured and been depicted, first in drawings and then in writing. On the rock walls of certain caves in southern Africa there are drawings of what look, to the expert eye, uncommonly like skins and pots for holding wine. The face, posture and gait of some of the human beings portrayed in these early ochred works of art can only be interpreted as reflecting a fair degree of bibulosity. Later, when writing developed, liquor became the subject of a good deal of early literature, including, as recent ground-breaking research by leading limericologists shows, primitive forms of the limerick so well known today.

A bibulous fellow in Dowa
was renowned as a great party-goer.
His every day was spent,
though never in Lent,
in drinking vast quantities of *moa*.

A barmaid who sold drinks at Liwonde
was known to her clients as Sweet Blondie.
When viewed from the river
she caused many a quiver
as she relaxed in the sun on the *khonde*.

The Tamarind Bar at Balaka,
when awarded the Carlsberg Green Charter,
took an unwise chance
and opened a branch
up the line at old Ntakataka.

An amorous young man from Mbame
set out one evening to charm me.
We went out to dine
and after some wine
he suggested a dish of salami.

A besotted old soak from Kumpasu
was addicted, I fear, to *kachasu.*
He once said 'How I love you'
to a great pink *njobvu*
as the tears streamed down from his *maso.*

An entrepreneurial colleague from Nsanje
made a wine he called *Vin Franjipanji.*
He became a man of great wealth
and when I asked of his health
he replied 'I'm fine, my friend. *Muli bwanji*?'

ooo ☺ ☻ ooo

THE X-RAY

The many friends of one of the Assistant Secretaries in the secretariat – a popular man, not least of all with the ladies - were deeply concerned when they learned that he had been taken to hospital. He had been suffering for some time from loss of balance - not an uncommon failing at the time, commented the less charitable observers of the capital's social life. The doctor diagnosed an infection of the inner ear and treated him accordingly. The treatment would take a few days to take effect but he was convinced that it would be successful. In the meantime, however – just to make sure – he decided to take an x-ray of the patient's skull. To his grave consternation, and that of his colleagues, when the doctor studied the x-ray it revealed a distinct and ominous dark patch in the lower right corner of the patient's brain. The patch puzzled and worried the doctor for several days until - prompted by his patient - he discovered that the x-ray negative had been carried to the radiology laboratory by a messenger who had that morning been paid his monthly salary. As was the custom at the time, he had 'signed' the pay sheet with his right thumb print and the black ink which was used was not yet fully dry.

COLONIAL SERVICE RECRUITMENT

A cadet washes bottles for those who are themselves merely junior bottle-washers. Not that this should unduly discourage you. All Civil Servants, of whatever seniority, are bottle-washers of one degree or another

Sir Arthur Grimble.

Recruitment to the British Colonial Service was always guided by a philosophy as to the sort of person the recruiters were looking for, the type of person, usually men, who in their view the colonies needed. In many cases - probably most - the actual candidates for appointment were unaware of the nature of this philosophy and indeed, if asked, would have been astonished to learn that there was any philosophy at all.

I

In a long letter to the Secretary of the British South Africa Company, on October 22nd, 1892, Harry Johnston, the Commissioner and Consul General of British Central Africa, asked the Company to recruit for him a barrister and at least two other officers, possibly a total of six. His letter also contained stipulations as to character, morality and marriage. The letter reveals some of the philosophy that Johnston, whether knowingly or not, used to guide his selection of the men to serve under him.

His recruits had to be aged between 21 and 35 years when they joined the Administration, and in health they had to be of 'good physique and thoroughly, absolutely sound and healthy.' So far as education was concerned they needed to be 'able to write in a good clear handwriting grammatical English, accurately spelt', and to be 'good arithmeticians, with some knowledge of law.' He was prepared, also, to pay allowances to officers with special skills and knowledge, for example: 'efficiency in geographical surveying with instruments'; 'certified competency in geology and mineralogy'; 'being conversant with forestry and botany'; having expertise in 'farriery and stock rearing and breeding, with a dash of the veterinary'; and possessing 'a thorough knowledge of the Portuguese, Hindustani, Swahili or Arabic, Chinyanja, Chiyao or Chibemba' languages. Police Officers had to show that after one year's service they 'possessed a fair knowledge of either Swahili, Arabic, Hindustani or the local African language.' Other allowances were paid to 'engineers able to construct roads, bridges, public works, etc.'; 'those who have studied law and are sufficiently well grounded to become magistrates'; 'those selected few who have previously been in military service and are judged capable to take up commands in the British Central Africa Police'; and 'qualified surgeons or doctors of medicine.' In essence, he was looking for men of good education with one or another technical skill.

As to character, Johnston was adamant that his recruits 'must be of unblemished character; smart, intelligent, cleanly, cheerful, civil and honest.' Any officer dismissed for blameworthy conduct before the end of a year's service had to repay half the passage fare incurred when he came out to Africa. The Commissioner much preferred his men to be teetotallers: 'No one with alcoholic weakness must be engaged. Africa is simply fatal to people who indulge in alcoholic stimulants except those taken very cautiously and seldom. No man with a tendency to 'drink' should come out to Tropical Africa.' He wanted his officers to be 'thoroughly gentlemanly, pleasant, self respecting, manly and yet neither too boisterous nor too athletic.' He also set out at length his views on 'the morality question':

> I wish it most clearly to be understood that I expect a very high level of decent behaviour from all serving with or under me in British Central Africa. I don't lay down the law for traders and others with no sense of responsibility. I merely point out that persons serving the British Central Africa Administration must not lead openly immoral lives.

Typically, he did not let his own then unmarried state prevent him from dilating 'in regard to marriage':

> The Missionaries' wives are really good women … like Mrs. Laws of Bandawe, whose influence is valuable in the country. I do not see in time, when things are a little more comfortable and settled, why our civil servants should not marry and have their wives out here and live with them. Don't for one moment sneer at this. An educated comely English woman with pleasant gifts and useful acquirements who will consent to come out, conceive and bring forth three English babies on the shores of Tanganyika deserves a tribute of respect from all Englishmen interested in the spread of their Empire.

On the subject of health Johnston went into extraordinary and now amusing detail, adding in parenthesis: 'Doctors' certificates are rarely honest and count for nothing':

> The complexion and healthiness of a man can be better told by a glance at his eyes, complexion and tongue, and by the feel of his hands than by reference to a Doctor's report. The eye must be bright, the complexion clear and wholesome (and this can be distinguished under surface disfigurement such as smallpox marks, which count for nothing), the tongue clean, well shaped, and pleasantly red, and the hands must be dry, warmish and firm. A man possessing these good traits can't have much the matter with him. As regards constitution and physique, fat men are absolutely unsuited for work in Africa.

With such very high standards and expectations, Johnston must have been disappointed when some fell short of the paragon to which he aspired in his civil servants.

II

Later recruiters also searched for the paragon. For the whole of the period from 1910 to 1950, the selection of Colonial Service officers was dominated by the views and practices of Sir Ralph Furse, Secretary to the Colonial Service Appointments Board. In his memoirs, *Aucuparius,* without being explicit, he reveals what his philosophy was as to the sort of man he felt the colonial service needed. Placing great emphasis on the interview, he wrote about his technique in assessing an applicant's suitability for Crown service in the British colonies:

> Our routine technique was briefly this. A man's application came in (it had to be in his own handwriting) with testimonials, references, and a photograph. You looked for any clues to be found in these and in the way he set out the information asked for on his form. Open testimonials were less valuable in themselves than as guides to further inquiries. You read these, and when - but only when - you had enough information to make an interview profitable did you ask him to call. By this time you knew quite a lot about his education and what he had made of it; his subsequent career, if any; his tastes and interests; what chance he had had of exercising responsibility or of showing in practice whether he possessed other qualities you were on the look-out for - self-reliance, for instance, self-sufficiency in loneliness, foresight, imaginative sympathy, or many others. In any case you had a good idea of where you wanted to probe further at the interview. An interview before you have got so far is of little

> value. Interviewing is an art and there is not much that one can usefully say about it: you will learn more about painting by looking at pictures than by reading art criticism.

Furse was clear that interviews demanded 'all that the interviewer can give.' And he added that 'every sense and faculty must be awake and concentrated, as in making love, on the business of apprehension', and that at the end of two or three interviews - he found four in a day the maximum for effective results - any interviewer worth his salt should feel exhausted. 'Like a tracker you must not neglect the slightest clue.' He gave three examples:

> A candidate was nearing the end of a very successful interview and I had practically decided to take him, when a telephone bell under my desk rang. I glanced at him and thought he started more than he need have. So I went back and took him through his record again. Close questioning revealed a point that had not so far come out: he had once been buried by a shell burst. I sent him for special examination by a neurologist, who advised that he might break down in the tropics.
>
> Then there was a very intelligent and able young man who on coming in gave me the tips of his fingers in a languid handshake. The interview revealed nothing against him, but those limp fingers worried me. We were considering him for Palestine where intelligence was certainly needed but so was toughness. When he hung out his fingers to say good-bye I slipped my hand forward and gripped his whole hand. His palm was as hard as nails. I put him in and he proved a success.
>
> Take, again, the case of an important senior vacancy. One candidate stood out but I wondered if he had enough patience. I arranged a further interview not long before he would have to catch a train for an important appointment in the north. I found out the time of his train, and, without telling him, arranged for a taxi to be ready just early enough to catch it. Then I prolonged the interview and watched him get more and more worried. But he controlled himself admirably. At last I said, 'You'll catch your train: I've got a taxi waiting.' We selected him, and he did brilliantly until his untimely death.

Furse recognised that every interviewer had his own technique. In his case, at interview boards he learnt more through his eyes than his ears, and he let his fellow interviewer colleagues do the talking, while he watched the candidate and put an occasional question to him.

Personal interviews were different and he had to put many questions to the candidate, but even so he let the interviewee talk as much as he would, and while Furse spoke to him about the Colonial Service - stuff he 'could say in his sleep' - he watched the candidate and his reactions, though he sometimes pretended to be looking at the ceiling. He felt that interviewing had affinities with portrait painting, and he had some sympathy with Augustus John's remark, 'The exploration of character should be left with confidence to the eye alone. Heaven knows what it may discover!' Furse, however, also allowed his ear to play an important role, but this took time: 'A man will not reveal himself till he is at ease and natural.' This was one of several reasons he had against interview by boards alone.

> Before a board a man is seldom quite himself: I have often proved this by watching a man before a board whom I had previously seen alone. But the combination of board and personal interview is valuable. It serves as a useful check, and tells you both what a man is really like and how he will behave in public. Normally he comes in all strung up and on the defensive: you must give him time to relax before you can really begin. The more I learnt of the business the longer my interviews lasted - at first perhaps a quarter of an hour; towards the end of my time three-quarters, an hour, an hour and a half. Beware of the fellow who says he can judge a man as soon as he comes into the room: he is probably lazy or does not know his job. It can be done sometimes, but rarely. Often you must correct your early impressions.

III

There are a number of interesting similarities in the philosophy of Colonial Service recruitment used by Johnston and that by Furse. Since between them they covered far and away the greater part of the colonial era from the 1890s it may be assumed that where their views coincide they represented the British Government's philosophy, albeit implied rather than expressed, that guided them in recruiting officers to the Service, at least so far as members of the Administration are concerned. There does not seem to be any reason to suppose that the recruiters basically looked for anything greatly different in professional and technical officers.

Both men had an abundant confidence in their own ability to pick the right sort of men, and both deployed a number of eccentric personal approaches to their techniques. Johnston placed great store on a man's bright eyes, clear and wholesome complexion, clean and well-shaped tongue, dry, warm and firm hands, and limited weight. Furse, too, was impressed by a candidate returning his hefty handshake with a palm that was as hard as nails. Little did later recruits suspect that when the consultant physician to the Colonial Office examined their throat he might surreptitiously be observing the cleanliness, shape and colour of their tongue, or in taking their pulse that he might be passing silent judgement on the dryness, warmth and firmness of their hands. What stayed most clearly in the memories of many of them was the ambiguous puzzled look on the face of the consultant physician as he studied the naked, full frontal specimen standing before him in his Harley Street consulting rooms.

Although both Furse and Johnston placed great faith in their individual ability to assess a candidate, the latter acted solely on his own ability whereas the former was obliged to involve a board of interviewers. Furse was cautious of 'the fellow who says he can judge a man as soon as he comes into the room' but Johnston would have had few such reservations: he was traditionally quick to assess a man's worth, whether accurately or not, and he was reluctant to modify his initial impressions. This certainly was not because he was lazy or did not know his job. Whilst Johnston might accept that 'every sense and faculty must be awake and concentrated' on the business of understanding, he would not have likened it to 'making love'. He was a bachelor until after he left British Central Africa. He did not marry Winifred Irby, step-daughter of the Head of the Africa Department in the Foreign Office, until he was almost forty, and he had no children. Indeed, he may not have understood the term 'making love', though he thought that in the course of time it would be good if 'educated comely English women with pleasant gifts and useful acquirements' agreed to coming to British Central Africa, 'conceive and bring forth three English babies.' He did not explain why he thought there should be three children, no more and no fewer; nor why they should be conceived and brought forth on the shores of Lake Tanganyika. They would not be the only children to have been conceived – though fewer would have been brought forth – on the quiet, warm, sandy, palm tree shaded beaches of Central African lakes.

Johnston would have agreed with Furse that a successful candidate needed to be self-reliant, self-sufficient in loneliness and have foresight, but it is unlikely that he would have understood what Furse was on about when he spoke of 'imaginative sympathy'.

Neither recruiter was inclined to trust the written opinion of others, in Johnston's case, a medical report, and in Furse's case solicited testimonials and open references save as a guide to further enquiries. Both relied on eye and ear; Furse made this explicit and Johnston's implied it: how else would he be able to assess the worth of a man's tongue, eyes, hands and complexion? He was an accomplished artist who, since his results were often considered to be 'too photographic', must have relied greatly on his eyes rather than imagination. Both were keen on a candidate's good handwriting.

Johnston specifically looked for skills and expertise - in surveying, geology, forestry, botany, farriery, stock rearing and breeding, languages, civil engineering and law - whereas by the time candidates appeared before Furse their professional training could be assumed. Johnston needed to be specific because he was on the whole recruiting generalist officers who, whilst becoming Jacks of all trades needed, in many cases, to be master of at least one of them. None the less, Furse was interested in a man's 'tastes and interests'. He looked, too, for what chance a candidate had had of exercising responsibility, whilst Johnston narrowed the field to 'those selected few' who had previous experience in military service and were consequently capable of taking up positions of command in the Police.

Though both expected good handwriting, as the years passed this became less important - as typewriters became more common - and probably less able to fulfil as handwriting deteriorated. Furse could assume acceptable arithmetic in the candidates who were increasingly better educated, but Johnston could not, and one of the main tasks of his generalist administrators was to keep the books. Many of the differences between the type of men Johnston and Furse were looking for were reflections of the changing tasks that colonial officers had to undertake and, with the passage of time, the changing conditions in which they worked. Law and order, for example, became tempered by the requirements of development and trusteeship, hence Furse's emphasis on patience and sympathy.

IV

Johnston and Furse were probably not conscious of working to a philosophy, and it is even less likely that the candidates themselves were aware – indeed they were almost certainly totally unaware – that they were being assessed against a philosophical back cloth. One such candidate has recorded his recollections of the manner in which he was recruited to the Colonial Administrative Service, in the early 1950s. He had to complete the application form in his own handwriting but there was no check made on his arithmetical ability. The form asked questions about his academic accomplishments – for which a small space was provided – and about such things as membership of school sports teams, offices held such as being a prefect, house captain or head boy – for which, significantly, a very much larger space was provided, embarrassingly large if one's only distinction was to have been the class milk monitor in the second form. There was also a parallel vetting exercise in which written references were secured from people who had been able to observe one's character and progress over the years: teachers, tutors, Scout leaders, clergymen, policemen and Commanding Officers if one had been in the armed services or had done national service. Once these documents had been studied at the Colonial Office there was a series of four interviews.

The first two interviews seemed designed to *dissuade* candidates from even remotely contemplating a job in the Service. The interviewer pointed out the numerous disadvantages: the dangers to health; the wild animals and the creepy-crawlies; the gravely limited diet; the primitive living conditions; the absence of one's children at school in Britain; the constant posting from one station to another with no reason being given; and the boredom faced in out-of-the-way places by one's wife – and, more dangerously, they added mysteriously, other people's wives. Leisure activities were discussed. 'So, you like opera?' 'I'm afraid you'll have to manage without that, old chap.' 'Reading?' 'Termites eat the books, old boy.' 'What about card games?' 'They eat cards too.' 'Landscape painting, maybe?' 'In that sun?' 'Swimming, possibly?' 'You've never heard of Bill Harris?' – their term for bilharzia. 'Cricket?' 'On a one man station? Dear oh dear.' And so on.

If one were still interested in the job there was a third interview. In this, the nature of the Administration's work was explained, one's reaction was sought and assessed, and one was encouraged to ask questions. Curiously, independence was not mentioned at any of the interviews. Four years later Ghana became independent, and within a decade virtually the whole of Africa.

Then came the final interview board, and the candidate later recalled only two questions. He was asked if he thought it better for a country to be governed badly by itself or well by foreigners. At that time - having been brought up on Pope's 'What 'ere is best administered is best' ideas - he thought good government was a self-evident value and said so. He immediately realized that this was a dangerous answer, and was relieved when the interviewer did not pursue the matter straightaway. The interviewer did return to it at the very end of the interview when, after a worrying pause, he simply asked if the candidate would wish to reconsider his earlier answer. He said yes he would, and it was left at that. In later life it seemed clear to him that there is no such thing as *good* government, only *bad* government. By this time he had studied O'Sullivan's conclusion that 'All government is evil and the parent of evil', though he conceded that some governments are worse than others.

The other question followed enquiries about the school he had been to. 'I take it you rode there?' Now, did he mean rode horses or did he mean rowed boats? He must have detected the candidate's hesitation, and rather impatiently added. 'Yes, *rowed.* I take it you *rode* there?' The candidate still didn't know, and lamely replied that he had *not*, though he *had* played first eleven cricket, soccer and hockey. He hoped that these might make up for having steered clear of both boats and horses. He left the interview, convinced they would never offer him a job. After all, you couldn't have chaps who not only thought perpetual domination by a foreign power was OK but neither rode a horse nor rowed a boat.

He was weighing up the few pros and the many cons of accepting a job in an overseas bank that had been offered to him, when, one evening, he received a telephone call from a little man in the Colonial Office – at least he sounded a little man on the telephone - to say a telegram would reach him the next day, offering him the post of administrative officer cadet in Nyasaland. He had never heard of Nyasaland, and he thought the Colonial Office man had said Iceland. So, being young and almost a graduate in Geography, he chanced the remark that he didn't know the country belonged to Britain and that it sounded a damned cold place for a colony. 'Young man', came the haughty reply, 'frivolity will get you nowhere.' Subsequent experience taught him that the man was right. Despite his surprise that he should be thought frivolous to consider Iceland a cold country and that it might be a British colony, he accepted the job and rested well that night, no longer deprived of sleep wondering how he was to earn his living and spend his future. He was comforted later when, shortly, he told the Professor of Geography he had accepted a job in Nyasaland. The Professor - a gentle man nearing the end of his career - smiled, looked thoughtful, and said, 'Nyasaland. Um. Nyasaland? Oh. Nyasaland you say? Ah, yes, Nyasaland. Well there it is then.' Clearly, he too had never heard of the place - or perhaps he thought his student also had said Iceland.

The young man graduated and, at the Colonial Office's expense, he spent an academic year in London, partly at the London School of Economics and Political Science, and partly at the School of Oriental and African Studies. At the former of these august institutions he was taught some colonial geography and history, some law, some economics and something about colonial constitutions. At the first geography class, the lecturer, a Doctor Morgan, introduced himself and said,

> Gentlemen, it is only fair that you should know that I am a specialist in the geography of the Soviet Union. Of the British colonies, and Africa in particular, I know nothing. Yet in their unfathomable wisdom your masters at the Colonial Office and my masters here at

> the London School of Economics and Political Science have ordained that I should address you on the no doubt intriguing subject of the geography of Africa. Gentlemen, Africa, as I understand it, lies somewhat to the east of the Atlantic Ocean and to the west of the Indian Ocean – or is it the other way round?

At the latter institution, the School of Oriental and African Studies, much more valuably in his view, one was taught the main language of the country to which one was to be posted, in his case Chinyanja. In addition, there were some amusing lectures on elementary bridge building, given at the Colonial Service Club in Tavistock Square by a retired Provincial Commissioner from Tanganyika who had built many bridges in the course of his long career. He was a great believer in the efficacy of visual aids, and illustrated his lectures by drawing with sticks of charcoal on a copy of the previous day's *Times* newspaper. He believed also that it was important to teach the wives of African chiefs how to knit, on the now unacceptable grounds that it gave them something to think about while they were talking. Ever since then, on visits to art galleries, the then young man has searched the descriptions of paintings, hoping to find among those that are labelled 'oil on canvas', 'water colour on card' and 'acrylic on board', one, just one, labelled 'charcoal on *Times*' - but always in vain. Of the London training year he found that only the tuition in languages was unequivocally valuable, but even then, an incident soon after he arrived in Nyasaland is revealing. He attended a Remembrance Day Service at which the Bishop of Nyasaland, a saintly, barefooted man, read the Lord's prayer in what he thought was Chinyanja, only to be told that his Grace had done so in Latin.

ooo ☺ ☻ ooo

THE STATIONERY REQUISITION

Dear Blanchard, too much string. Yours, C.D

Charles Dickens to a young poet, Laman Blanchard, who had submitted to him a collection of verses entitled 'Orient Pearls at Random Strung'

In his early days in the Administration, a young officer was given the routine task of ordering the office sundries. This superficially simple task was complicated by the requirement that each item be precisely specified by reference to a complex catalogue of available stores and supplies. It required that items be identified by the class and sub-class reference number and then entered on an almost as complicated requisition form. The young officer laboured mightily over the catalogue, parts of which were beyond his comprehension, try as he might to understand. He waited with trepidation for the stores to arrive at the *boma* or, alternatively and more likely in his view, for a sharp letter to be received saying that he had made a thorough mess of the whole affair. In the event, he was relieved when, several weeks later, a large box of stationery arrived. He checked each item against his requisition list and was delighted to see that every item and its reference number had been ticked off. All save one: 'parcel string'. Tucked inside the box was a letter signed by the Controller of Stores, which read: 'Ref. your requisition for one hundred yards of parcel string for which the correct reference number is 12345/ABC. You ordered number 67890/DEF which is the reference number for hangman's rope. Do you intend to hang the whole adult male population of your District?

ooo ☺ ☻ ooo

THE BRIDGE

Now who will stand on either hand
and keep the bridge with me?
Macaulay.

Within a few days of arriving in Nyasaland, a brand new cadet was posted to take over a sub-district as Assistant District Commissioner in a low lying, hot area in the rift valley, twenty odd miles from Zomba, the country's miniscule but beautiful capital. The sub-district was a one-man station. There were no other expatriates and but a tiny handful of African officials. His predecessor was being transferred because his wife was pregnant and it was generally considered too unhealthy a place for expatriate babies to be born and brought up. He spent the night with them, and the next morning they got into their Land Rover, started the engine and were about to drive off when it suddenly dawned on him that he had no idea what he was supposed to do.

Like a drowning man whose life flashes before him, he mentally flicked through the notes from his London University pre-service course, but found no guidance. As the wheels of the Land Rover began to turn, he asked 'Wha … Wha ... What do I do?' Impatient to be on his way lest his wife give birth sooner than expected, for she was - as they say of ladies in her condition and of convicts awaiting execution – nearing her time, his predecessor cheerfully shouted, 'Build a bridge, old chap!' 'Where shall I build it?' he enquired as the Land Rover pulled away. His predecessor was becoming exasperated by his questions and replied, the new man thought somewhat irritably, above the din of the accelerating engine and through the cloud of red dust into which he was fast disappearing, 'For God's sake, man, there must be a bloody river around here somewhere.'

He was right, there *was* a river around there, and quite nearby. And what is more, the prospect of a bridge seemed to please the local villagers, who until then had to wade through the river in the rainy season. So, with the labourers who worked at the *boma*, he began to build a bridge across it. Its structure - drawn in the sand with a twig - was a stone wall buttress on each bank, across which would be placed the long, straight trunks of two bluegum trees. Upon the bluegums he would fix wooden planks. All this he felt he could manage. It was not a complicated affair. There was a good quantity of cement and adequate planking in the store, and rocks for the buttresses were close at hand.

What he had *not* contemplated was how the labourers were to be paid, nor indeed did the question cross his mind until the head, and only, clerk asked about their pay. He had no idea how they were to be paid. When he asked the clerk, he was told that his predecessor had filled in a yellow form, taken it up to Zomba to the Treasury Cashier's office where the Treasury Cashier would give him a cheque which he could cash at the bank, bring the money back and pay the labourers. He asked if the clerk was confident such an unlikely method would work. He was assured that it had worked with his predecessor and he saw no reason why, if they prayed hard enough, it should not work with him. And he was right. After much searching, they found a crumpled yellow form and ironed it smooth with a charcoal iron. He copied the previous month's entries, took it to the Cashier in Zomba, got the money at the bank, came back and paid the much relieved labourers. He also took the opportunity to ask the Treasury Cashier how *he* got paid, and he must have seen to that too, because a week or so later he received a cheque and was surprised and delighted to see his salary, agreed months before at £350 a year, had gone up to £525 a year - a 50% increase!

His visit to Zomba had other consequences. He went to the Gymkhana Club for a drink before returning to the heat of his sub-*boma*, and there he met a number of kindly gentlemen who asked who he was and how he was getting on. He told them about his bridge, and one gently asked, 'Have you been here in the rainy season?' He said no he hadn't and received the helpful advice, 'I'd put another foot or two on that bridge of yours if I were you.' The ADC took this advice and built the buttresses a couple of feet higher than originally intended.

Come the next monthly pay day and the ADC again visited Zomba, again was courteously assisted by the Treasury Cashier and again called in at the Club for a drink, where he met more kindly gentlemen who enquired after his health and his work. This time a different fellow drinker told him that it rained like hell down where he was living once the wet season started, and if he were the ADC - and he was very pleased indeed that he was *not* the ADC - he'd put another foot or so on the bridge to make sure the water didn't top it. Again, he took the advice, and after one more pay run to see the Treasury Cashier, the bank manager and the kindly gentlemen at the Club, the bridge towered above the surrounding landscape. He now had to build sloping causeways on each side of the river so that vehicles and pedestrians could climb up from the road to reach the bridge. It was completed just as the rains broke and lasted several years before it was swept downstream in a violent flood – though he never actually saw anyone using it.

ooo ☺ ☻ ooo

VOTER REGISTRATION

During the 1961 registration of voters for the country's first general election, at which one of the few requirements was that a voter should be literate – that is, able to read and correctly complete the registration form unaided - one of the registering officers was puzzled to see an old African lady turn the registration form upside down and proceed painstakingly to complete it with shaky writing that was also upside-down. So intrigued was the registration officer that he quietly enquired of her why she filled it in that way. Slightly embarrassed, she explained that this was the way she had practised copying it from the example given to her by her Malawi Congress Party tutor who had sat on the other side of the table from her. The registration officer concluded that this was evidence not simply of literacy but of very high quality literacy, and he had no hesitation in registering her.

ooo ☺ ☻ ooo

PRACTISING MEDICINE

The doctor is especially dangerous when poor.
Shaw.

The bridge was just one of the happenings in his sub-district that our brand new cadet had not anticipated. He had not been there more than a few days when the local dispenser, the only source of medical assistance for many miles around, ran away and was never seen again. Why he absconded he did not know. In any case, he was left to run the dispensary, the local clinic, and minister to those who, in decreasing numbers, sought his aid. He had always been squeamish about blood and pain, whether his or others', yet he had no alternative but to suppress his retching and steel himself against the sight of the blood, puss and dirty wounds that came before him each morning.

He shoved all the stainless steel instruments into a drawer - he was steering clear of surgery and midwifery. There were several bottles of medicaments on the shelves, and he put away all those whose purpose was not clear to him, leaving only a small bottle labelled 'Ear Drops', a large unlabelled bottle of bright yellow liquid, which he recognized as acriflavine, and an equally large unlabelled bottle of bright purple liquid, which he recognized as gentian violet. He knew that both acriflavine and gentian violet were antiseptics, but what the difference was he did not know. So on Mondays, Wednesdays and Fridays he used the former and these became known as yellow days, and on Tuesdays, Thursdays and Saturdays he used the latter and they became known as purple days.

Two cases long stayed in his memory. The first concerned an elderly village headman who came to him one morning and said that a wild animal had spent several days in his ear, and although it had now gone his ear was still sore. The ADC had not yet learned that the same word could be used for insect and wild animal, but since it had gone it didn't seem to matter. 'Ah Ha,' he said to himself, 'at least in this case I have a remedy.' He took down the bottle marked Ear Drops, asked the headman to tilt his head to one side and gently poured a few drops into his upturned ear. To his alarm he yelled like a wounded buffalo and fled from the dispensary, his white robes flowing behind him. Several others left with him. He was never seen again. Later, when mentioning this apparent lack of gratitude to a doctor, the ADC was asked if he had diluted the ear drops and had to confess that he had not. The Doctor assured him that he had done no lasting harm.

The other case had a happier and more rewarding ending. A young mother brought her small child of about a year, maybe fifteen months, to see him in the dispensary one morning. The child had fallen onto an open kitchen fire and badly burned its buttocks. The ADC cleaned the wound and, because it was a yellow day, he bathed it in acriflavine. Since she brought the baby every day for checking, the wound was treated alternately with yellow antiseptic and purple antiseptic. He later felt that this case disproved Archbishop Desmond Tutu's claim that it was he who had invented the term 'the rainbow people'. As the weeks passed, the raw wound got smaller and smaller as the surrounding skin began to cover it, first pink and then its normal dark brown. He was lucky the treatment worked, and he still places this minor miracle near the top of his short list of successes in life.

There were two other incidents that came his way that were connected with medicine, or rather with that branch of medicine in which many observers have been utterly unable to distinguish doctor from patient: psychiatry. In the first of these a man came to see him and asked him to lock up his son. He asked what the son had done wrong and was told he had done nothing wrong, but every full moon he went insane and became extremely violent, a danger to himself and others. This, the ADC thought, was an unlikely yarn but he agreed to see the boy. He turned out to be a good looking, healthy, sensible young man. They talked for a while and the lad told him that yes, every time there was a full moon he ran amok and caused great harm to all near him. He really did think the ADC should lock him up. After all, the cell in the local court house was rarely used and he would need it for only a short time each month. The ADC agreed, with some reluctance.

So, a day or so before the next full moon, he came along with his family, carrying between them a very heavy log of wood, forked at one end - the sort used in the olden days as a slave stick, but much heavier. In the cell at the court, the family placed the forked end round his neck and secured it with rope, so as to restrain him. They stayed with him until the full moon had passed, then thanked the ADC and returned to their village. They looked forward to seeing him in a month's time. The young man seemed quite normal again, but on the ADC's visits in the meantime there is no doubt that he had gone berserk. His only worry was that he vaguely recalled one of the law lecturers in London saying something about writs of *habeas corpus* and the dire penalties for unlawful detention.

The second case concerned the young clerk at the same local court. He came to see the ADC and asked to be allowed to take six months' leave, starting straight away. The ADC said he couldn't do this unless he was able to give him a very good reason for being absent for so long and so urgently. The clerk was reluctant, but eventually he explained that his wife had given birth to their first baby a few weeks earlier and he had broken the taboo that forbade him sleeping with his wife until the baby was six months old. Having broken this taboo it was inevitable that he would be struck down by a disease in which one lost one's colouring and one's body wasted away. The only cure for this lay in the hands of a witchdoctor whom he needed to consult urgently and who would prescribe the necessary remedy. It would take several months to work, and without it he would assuredly soon be dead. The ADC told him he would need a while to consider this and to decide how his work was to be done in his absence. He asked some of the elders about this story and none of them seemed in the least bit surprised, though they did mutter about the young nowadays breaking taboos.

A few days later the ADC went to tell the clerk that he agreed to his absence and he could go straightaway. To his horror he found that the clerk's skin had turned a pale grey and that his hair was pure white in colour and, short though it was, was literally standing on end. The ADC hoped that his eyes were deceiving him but they weren't. The clerk left immediately, and the ADC handed over his work to a temporary replacement. Some four or five months later he returned, his skin was its normal healthy brown, his hair was black and curly. He was in excellent health again. He brought his wife - a very pretty young lady - and his baby daughter with him. They looked enormously happy and told the ADC they were expecting a second baby; this time they would be more careful to follow custom.

ooo ☺ ☻ ooo

THE ROOF BEAM

Just after the First World War, the British Government encouraged Europeans, including ex-army officers, to take up tobacco planting in Nyasaland. The encouragement included granting leases of estate land and proved sufficiently successful as to attract several aspirant estate owners. Among these were two Scotsmen, MacNab and Maxwell who settled on neighbouring estates in the Southern Province. They became close friends but were also keen rivals. The rivalry manifested itself most clearly in the competitive way in which they built their respective estate houses, their homes. Where one excelled in the size of his sitting room, the other beat him in the dimensions of his master bedroom. Their kitchens were almost identical and one could not detect any qualitative difference between their verandahs. Where one would take a step forward the other would counter-attack with an equally impressive step. There was nothing between the two houses, save in one respect: the main roof beam across the ceiling of the sitting room. By felling two large trees, sawing them into timbers with twelve inch square cross sections and getting a carpenter, under very close supervision, to join then neatly and securely, MacNab crowned his room with a single, unbroken span. The roof no longer needed a pillar in the centre to support it, and the sitting room consequently became much more spacious. At long last he had bested his friend. Maxwell grudgingly admitted defeat.

A year or so later, still narked by his compatriot's success, Maxwell was trudging through a well wooded, remote part of his estate, when he came across the tallest and most robust *mbawa* tree he had ever seen. It was a monster. Scarcely able to contain his glee, he determined to get his revenge on his neighbour, but he knew that he would have to tread cautiously for he considered MacNab not to be beyond a few dirty tricks in order to maintain the supremacy he had achieved with his single-span roof beam. To avoid the danger of discovery and sabotage, Maxwell arranged for those he entrusted with felling the tree to be sworn to secrecy and bribed with promises of a great beer-drink when the job was fully completed. He waited until MacNab went off on one of his hunting trips and then, with two wagons pulled by a dozen oxen, he had the tree, shorn of its branches, hauled to the compound next to his house. The tree trunk was laid out on trestles – no mean feat in itself – and was then enclosed in a high grass fence so that the work on it could not be observed by others, especially those from MacNab's estate. Over the next several months the trunk was adzed, shaved and crafted into an enormous length of timber, perfectly straight, immaculate in the shape of its twelve inch square cross section and rich in the reddy-brownness of its colouring. Though, slightly to his regret, the overall length of the beam would not be any greater than MacNab's, it would be an utterly unprecedented and mightily impressive single piece of timber, enough to make any rival green with envy, livid with anger and puce with fury. During this long period of preparation, Maxwell visited his neighbour much less frequently than in the past, fearing that after the customary drinks, he would let slip news of what he had afoot. MacNab was suspicious but attributed the cooler relationships to Maxwell's continued umbrage.

At last the timber was ready to be installed over Maxwell's sitting room. He gave sedulously detailed instructions to the carpenter who was to supervise its installation and repeated them. Much to his regret he would be unable to supervise the operation himself because the curing of his tobacco crop had reached a critical stage and necessitated his presence at the barns for whole days at a time. This did not disturb him too much because his carpenter was a careful man, had been in his employ for many years and had always completely understood his working instructions and carried them out faithfully. He had received his primary school education at a Church of Scotland school and as a consequence had the distinct advantage of understanding what his employer was saying – much better than did the English ex-army officers on other estates in the area. As an extra precaution Maxwell found an excuse to visit MacNab's house with his carpenter while the owner was away on another hunting trip, and to show him exactly how he wished the carpenter to install the new beam. The carpenter studied the room and the supporting beam carefully. 'You want me to remove the pillar in the centre of the room and install the new beam exactly like *Bwana* MacNab's?' 'Aye, just like the *Bwana*'s. But be careful how you remove the pillar and how you lift the beam – it's very heavy.' Still chuckling with delight, he went off to supervise the curing in the tobacco barns.

When he returned to his house late that afternoon, rubbing his hands with the delightful prospect of viewing for the first time his sitting room crowned with its magnificent beam, manifestly outstandingly superior to that in his neighbour's dwelling, as would be clear to all visitors - and he intended that there should be many of these to observe the fruits of his victory. The carpenter was waiting for him on the verandah, smiling proudly at the end of a good day's work and looking forward to the promised beer-drink. 'How has the work gone?' he asked confidently. 'Is the beam safely installed?' 'Yes, *Bwana*', came the reply. 'Taking down the pillar was a bit of a problem, but putting up the beam was fine and we did it exactly like *Bwana* MacNab's, as you wanted it.'

Triumphantly, Maxwell entered the sitting room, blinking after coming in from the sunlight. As his eyes became accustomed to the light and he began to examine the full glory of the new beam, he let out an anguished roar, like a mortally wounded buffalo, that struck puzzlement and fear in equal proportions into the carpenter. His magnificent single length beam had been sawn in two, and neatly joined to make a single span – just like *Bwana* MacNab's!

ooo ☺ ☻ ooo

STATE OF EMERGENCY

Just after midnight, on 3 March 1959, the Governor of Nyasaland declared a state of emergency over the whole of the country, in which the first step was to arrest as many as possible of the chairmen and secretaries of the Nyasaland African Congress who had attended an alleged 'murder plot' meeting near Blantyre five weeks earlier. These arrests were to be made at dawn under the supervision of Administrative Officers, assisted by police officers and officers from departmental staff acting as Special Constables. In a District of the Southern Province the District Commissioner's task was to arrest a Village Headman whose home was in a low lying part of the Shire plain, a few miles from the foot of the escarpment. He was accompanied by an Assistant District Commissioner, a Police Inspector and a messenger.

They drove from the *boma* in an open-back Land Rover. The road zigzagged down the escarpment to the Shire Valley and, having learned a lesson from the 1953 disturbances, when other arrests had been made, they drove in complete darkness so that their headlights should not be seen from the valley below. They arrived just as dawn was breaking.

To the extent that four men can surround a house, they surrounded the Village Headman's house, the usual mud and wattle construction under a grass thatch roof. Everything was quiet. The DC approached and knocked on the door, calling '*Odi*' as he did so. There was the sound of shuffling in the house and the door was eventually opened by the Village Headman's wife, who not unnaturally was surprised and frightened by their early morning visit. The DC explained briefly what their purpose was and entered the house. He looked carefully in each of the few rooms but there was no sign of the Village Headman, and his wife was reluctant to tell them where he was. They had also been instructed to search for and seize any documents which might contain information useful to the special branch investigators, especially about the 'murder plot' meeting. Concealed behind a door, hanging from a six inch nail, was an overcoat, the pockets of which bulged and might contain documents. In the pitch blackness – there was no lighting in the house – the DC took down the coat, and reached into the inside of it. As his hand was about to feel inside the pocket a large mouse jumped out, scurried up his arm and fled. He had rarely been so terrified in all his life and it took him some time to recover his composure.

His recovery was helped by the appearance of the Village Headman at the door, buttoning up the fly of his trousers and explaining that he had been for his usual early morning pee at the end of his garden. He was sorry he had been so occupied when they arrived and unable to greet them as courteously as he should have. The DC had the distinct impression that he was teasing his visitors; when he explained what they were doing, the headman gave the impression that he knew they were to call on him that morning and had consequently taken his early morning visit to his garden rather earlier and had taken rather longer about it than usual. He made no effort to resist his arrest but asked, since they were old friends and it was a cold morning and he would be travelling in the back of the Land Rover, that the DC should not handcuff him as he had been instructed. The DC readily agreed that only as they got very close to the *boma* and neared the prison, would he be handcuffed. The Village Headman promised to tell no one that the DC had disobeyed his instructions to handcuff him.

As they returned back up the escarpment, the DC was driving, the ADC was in the middle and the Inspector was in the near side seat. They were all tired, particularly the ADC, who dozed off. As he dozed, he fiddled absentmindedly with a tear gas grenade, one of three or four they had brought in case of trouble, and, nestling it on his lap, unknowingly began to unscrew the detonating mechanism. The Inspector and the DC noticed this simultaneously but only after the ADC had completely unscrewed it and was holding the grenade in his left hand and the mechanism with its pin and handle in his right. They knew that the way in which the grenade was activated was to remove the pin which released the handle and, clearly, they thought in their panic, since the handle was not only released but was actually removed from the grenade, the thing was bound to go off in seconds. The Inspector tore open the door and leapt out. The DC was inclined to do the same but since he was driving and was very close to the edge of the escarpment, he could not do so. Surprised that there was no explosion and release of tear gas, the DC slowed the vehicle down and only then realized that unscrewing the two halves of the grenade, far from activating it, in fact rendered it inoperable. He roundly cursed the ADC for alarming him and risking his driving the vehicle over the edge of the escarpment, but the ADC was still too sleepy to understand why they were so upset. The messenger and the Village Headman slept on unawares in the back of the vehicle.

ooo ☺ ☻ ooo

FROM A GREAT HEIGHT

What pleasure lives in height.
Tennyson.

Governor Kittermaster was an immensely tall man - he was six feet seven inches tall by the time he left school - and the story is told of a visit he made from Zomba to view game in the Luangwa valley of Northern Rhodesia. The District Commissioner of Fort Jameson had a camping site made for the visiting governor, complete with grass fence, flag pole, thatched kitchen, breakfast shelter and other facilities. He told the sergeant messenger, who was supervising the construction of this splendid camp, that he was about to meet the tallest man he would ever see. The sergeant was impressed and looked forward to the Governor's arrival. Sir Harold arrived during the afternoon, and after tea he visited the spacious grass and thatched *chimbuzi,* the lavatory, which, under the sergeant's supervision, had been constructed. As he entered, he was astonished to see that the seat of the *chimbuzi* had been built four feet off the ground!

ooo ☺ ☻ ooo

WATER SUPPLIES

One may not doubt that, somehow, good shall come of water.
Rupert Brooke.

I

At one of the districts in the western part of the Central Province there were six European families: the District Commissioner, the Police Superintendent, the Agricultural Officer, the Assistant District

Commissioner, the Executive Officer and the Inspector of Police. These are placed here roughly in order of their rank - or at least their perceived standing - within the Civil Service. Save in purely functional terms this hierarchy had little local relevance, except in one respect: the location of the houses which were allocated to them. It was the location rather than the quality of the houses which was important, for the District Commissioner's house, though newer, was, in terms of accommodation and space, not as good as some of the others.

The station lay on the lower slopes of a rather attractive mountain, and the government European housing area was on a gentle incline, with the DC's house at the top of the slope, significantly higher than the others, where it was slightly more secluded and where it enjoyed a better view from its verandah and the benefit of a cooler evening air. The other inhabitants did not seem to mind the DC having these advantages, and indeed they had their doubts about one aspect: the water supply.

The water was pumped from a bore hole and piped to a tank just above the DC's house. This was the obvious place to put the storage tank, so that water could flow under gravity from it to all the houses. However, such was the gradient, and such was the general inadequacy of the quantity of water in the tank, that the water flowed too quickly downhill, bypassing the DC's house and most plenteously supplying the bachelor Inspector of Police's dwelling, thereby reversing the order of precedence on the station and frequently leaving the DC and his family water-less. It was he who suffered most because it was his house that was significantly higher than those of his colleagues. The gradient between the other houses was not as great as that between the DC's house and his nearest neighbour, the Superintendent of Police.

To overcome the problem, the DC had a stopcock installed in the pipe between his house and the next, and he had the supply below his house turned off each evening just before bath time. Not unnaturally, the other families, deprived of water at the very time when they also wished to bathe, took umbrage, but rather than confront the DC directly – since he had not consulted them and it rarely paid to upset the DC - the Superintendent undertook to solve the problem clandestinely: he sent his houseboy each evening to creep through the bush and turn on the water. The DC suspected what was happening and as a counter measure built a small brick enclosure over the stopcock and secured it with a lock and a key which he entrusted to his head servant. A few more days enabled the Superintendent to obtain a copy of the key – it transpired later that his cook was the brother of the DC's head servant. There followed a period in which the DC instructed a *boma* messenger to patrol the general area of the stopcock each evening to prevent the water being turned on. The servants' daughters from one of the other houses then employed diversionary tactics to lure away the messenger while others crept on all fours through the bush and quickly turned on the tap.

The extraordinary thing was that relations between the DC and his family on the one hand, and his fellow officers and theirs on the other did not in the slightest deteriorate – presumably because both were confident of winning the battle – nor was the matter discussed between them. At least not until the Provincial Commissioner visited the station and stayed with his wife in the DC's guest house, the hot water supply of which, as with other houses, was unaffected by the turnings on and off of the stopcock since each house had its own hot water tank – an old petrol drum over a log fire - which filled slowly and at leisure.

On the first evening of the PC's visit, and after a day spent largely in walking fairly long distances in various parts of the District, the PC was looking forward, as was his wife, to a relaxing bath followed by a sundowner drinks party to which the DC had invited all the other families on the station. While the PC and his wife were getting their clothes ready, they ran the hot water for their bath, and when the bath was sufficiently filled with hot water they turned on the cold tap to lower the water to the correct temperature. To their surprise, no matter how fully they turned the tap, no cold water appeared. They had no choice other than either to wait until the bath water cooled down or to go without a bath. They decided on the former. They repeatedly tested the temperature and discovered that in addition to the old adage that a watched pot never boils, a boiling bath never cools – at least not nearly quickly enough. Their used day clothes had already been taken by the DC's houseboy to be washed and ironed, and they were reluctant to put on clean evening clothes over their unwashed bodies. Naked, they sat and waited for the water to cool, while the other guests arrived and awaited the PC. In the end, they risked the temperature, which was much higher than they normally had. Pink-fleshed and half an hour late, they joined the DC and his other guests. This was the first time that the problem of the station's water supply had been raised openly: the PC saw the funny side of the hot water debacle but his wife was significantly less amused. It took his visit and the bathing fiasco to solve the water management problem: an informal meeting between the DC and the Superintendent of Police in which they agreed that the stopcock should be only partially closed each evening so that every family received some water, even though it was in smaller quantities.

II

Administrative Officers who served under the governorship of Sir Geoffrey Colby in the late 1940s and early 1950s, when they were obliged to spend at least two weeks every month on *ulendo* and in practice spent more than two weeks in the bush, will long remember the pleasures awaiting them back at camp after a long and arduous day tramping around distant parts of their district. These pleasures typically included a quiet sit down under the fly sheet of their tent, enjoying first a cup of tea and a little later a cool sundowner drink. Pre-eminently they included a bath taken in either a shallow canvas contrivance or a metal contraption slightly more closely resembling those that folk in more sedentary professions would recognize as a bath. The water for these ablutions was drawn from local sources, usually a nearby stream, and was heated in various containers over an open log fire.

The invariable practice with virtually every expatriate family was that their drinking water – including the water with which they cleaned their teeth – was boiled and then filtered through a porous ceramic 'candle' fitted inside a pottery or metal container. In one of the districts of the Southern Province there served an Assistant District Commissioner of exceptional personal cleanliness, a cleanliness born of his paranoiac fear of catching some foul disease from his bath water. His wife attributed this fear to her husband having taken far too much to heart the warnings, uttered by the spinster matron at his prep school, of eternal and fiery damnation for those who peed in the bath. Whatever the cause, he determined that the high standard of hygiene applied to the preparation of his drinking water should be extended to the preparation of his bath water.

A former army officer, he recalled an exercise in which he had taken part many years earlier at the Royal Military Academy, Sandhurst, which involved calculating the various provisions that would be required by a team of men on a commando expedition. Deploying this nearly forgotten experience, he calculated the amount of bathing water that he would need for a fortnight's sojourn in the bush. The result was an alarming volume of water. Undeterred, and with the help of a tinsmith who had learned his trade while resident for many years on and off in the Central Prison at Zomba, he set up a row of twelve water filters on a plank above two thoroughly cleaned forty-four gallon fuel drums to which the taps on the filters were connected by funnels and hoses made from lengths of equally well cleansed bicycle inner tubes. He employed the cook's eldest son to man the whole operation and paid him above the normal wages for unskilled work, partly because he wished to ensure as far as he could that it was conducted properly, partly because there was no similar job that he knew of on which he could base a comparable salary, but mainly because he succumbed to the argument of his cook that the work was far from being unskilled.

The water-boy's job was to boil water in *debes* – old paraffin tins - or *supuliyas* – 'aluminium hollow ware' as the customs schedules had it - over an open fire outside the main kitchen of the ADC's house, and then pour it into the row of filters, topping them up regularly throughout the day. He left the taps of the filters open so that the boiled and filtered water ran continuously into the drums below. The ADC's calculations were impeccable and it took precisely fourteen days for two drums to be filled. These two were then sealed – to ensure that there was no tampering with their contents – and were placed ready to be taken in a Land Rover when the ADC started his next *ulendo*, while two others were placed in position ready to be filled while he was away, for use when the he was back at the *boma* and not on *ulendo*. The ADC carefully calibrated two new and previously unused broom handles as dip sticks in such a fashion that the level of the rising water as the drums were being filled at the station, and the level of it as they were being emptied on *ulendo*, could be measured. The operation was continuous, the water-boy sleeping next to the equipment so as to be able to top up the filters as they slowly emptied and so as to prevent the larceny of the precious water by any felonious and less self-enterprising individuals on the station. The water-boy was unique. There was no similar operator in the whole of the country – but then there was no similar *bwana* in the whole of the country either.

III

Committee Room No. 1 in the Legislative Assembly building was the venue of many important matters. It was here that Executive Council sat, where the Governor solemnly confirmed or commuted the death sentence passed on murderers by the High Court, and where, later, Dr. Banda's ministers first openly rebelled against him. It was also the meeting place of the Legislature's Standing Committee on Finance. This committee was a vital part of the constitution, for through it the Legislature attempted to curb and control the powers of the Executive in relation to raising and spending public money. Given such weighty matters as these, Committee Room No.1 was no place for levity, repartee, badinage, banter, hilarity or guffawing. Yet there was an occasion when the solemnity of the proceedings taking place in its sober interior was broken. And it was broken during a sitting of the Standing Committee on Finance.

Before dealing with the occasion in question, it is important to explain that the Committee members included all the non-official members of the Legislature and that the only other member was the Financial Secretary, a senior civil servant. This was in strict contrast to the position in the Legislature itself where officials, whether ex officio or nominated, heavily outnumbered the non-officials. It is not surprising that the non-official members of the Committee took the opportunity of its meetings to flex their muscles, exercise their powers to put the Government in its place and stop civil servants over-taxing the poor public and spending their money profligately. Although the Financial Secretary was on his own with no colleague to support him he knew more about the construction and detail of the draft budgets – through which revenue was raised and expenditure deployed – than anyone else present. Indeed he had overseen the drafting of it. He realized, however, how easily a belligerent, quick thinking and slick tongued non-official member might trip him up. Consequently, he always prepared himself assiduously – he personally preferred, and frequently used, the word 'sedulously' - and took with him an abundance of supporting papers.

At the meeting in question – that at which the traditional solemnity of the proceedings in Committee Room No.1 was seriously dented – the Committee followed its normal routine of discussing each Heading in the draft budget in turn in alphabetical order. Though several Headings took up a good deal of time, others were agreed without comment. They had reached the general area of public utilities such as water and electricity, and were getting through their business expeditiously when the Financial Secretary momentarily lost his place in the papers before him. Anxious not to miss anything, and being particularly interested in the public utilities, he raised his hand to attract the Chairman's attention. There followed a seven word exchange that had a uniquely devastating effect on the gravity of the proceedings. 'Mr. Chairman.' 'Yes?' 'Have we passed Water?'

ooo ☺ ☻ ooo

CHIEF JUSTICES – AND THEIR WIVES

I

From Tete on the Zambezi and other stopping places further south, a certain Nyasaland Chief Justice on his journeys to Southern Rhodesia or South Africa to attend Appeal Court hearings would post letters to his daughters at school in England. A caring father, he was anxious that they should receive regular correspondence from him. Consequently, he got his secretary to write and type letters from him, in advance, purporting to have been written by him, first at Tete, then Salisbury, then Beit Bridge, and so on. He was not only a caring parent but also a frugal father. So he got his secretary to keep used envelopes, carefully turn them inside out, address them to his daughters and seal the letters in them. All the CJ had to do then was to buy a local stamp and post the letters – tasks which he no doubt found tiresome and exhausting.

II

The charming and amusing wife of a different Chief Justice wrote to thank a junior civil servant for helping at a garden party at her home one Saturday afternoon. There were two entrances to the Chief Justice's official residence. Most people would arrive at the front entrance and the young civil servant was asked to collect tickets at the other. This he did, and on the following Monday was pleased to receive a delightful letter from the Chief Justice's wife in which she thanked him for so splendidly looking after her back entrance.

III

The KAR sergeant in charge of the guard at the main gate of Government House was surprised to see a large chauffer driven black car drive up to the gatehouse at half past six in the morning of New Year's Day. From the car emerged a well, and rather formally, dressed middle aged European man and woman. Their attire was completed with, in his case, a black bowler hat and tightly furled black umbrella, and, in her case, an Ascot Ladies Day hat and long sleeved gloves. The sergeant was puzzled by their arrival since he was aware that even those Europeans who had stayed up all night celebrating at the Gymkhana Club had already collapsed into their, or someone else's, bed. He was intrigued to see the couple creep stealthily up to the little sentry-box building in which the Governor's visitors' book was kept, and shortly emerge with what struck him as a rather aloof smile. They then left, sitting in the back seats of their limousine, not having said a word to him.

In the evening, when the Aide de Camp collected the visitors' book, he noticed that the very first signatures of the day – and there were few others - were those of the Chief Justice and his wife who had driven the forty plus miles from Blantyre, and that they had signed themselves, 'Sir X and Lady Y'. He of course knew that during that day the New Year's honours list had been published and that in it the Chief Justice had been knighted – only as a Knight Bachelor, a member of the Society of Knights Bachelor, he privately sniffed, and not as a Knight Commander of the Most Distinguished Order of St. Michael and St. George, but none the less a knight. Well versed in the protocol and etiquette of these matters, he also knew that a recipient of a knighthood should not assume the title 'Sir' nor correspondingly his wife the title 'Lady', until he had been dubbed. Consequently, he wrote to the Chief Justice and his wife, whom he correctly and pointedly addressed as 'Mr. and Mrs. Y', a letter enclosing a copy of the page from the protocol handbook of the orders of chivalry, which set out quite clearly - indeed the copy he sent dealt solely with the matter – that the title 'Sir' should not be used until the recipient had received the accolade from the Sovereign at the Palace, which might not be for several months – unless, of course, he would like the Governor on her behalf to confer it locally.

ooo ☺ ☻ ooo

THE HEAD CLERK

Some of the *boma* head clerks knew their districts backwards – the most senior and experienced of all the country's head clerks, for example. He had narrowly missed wrongfully being hanged after the Chilembwe Rising of 1915, and would say to the District Commissioner, when he asked where a particular village was, 'Sir, there is no such village in this district', knowing that the DC could not contradict him, otherwise he would not have asked him in the first place. He also would account for any files he could not find by saying with great solemnity, 'That European woman who was an Administrative Assistant here, and who undoubtedly usurped my authority, Sir, she burnt them.' It was he, too, who when the DC asked to see the births, deaths and marriage registers, eased himself up, lifted the cushion from his chair and produced them from where they had long been hidden; he reckoned that without them he would have terrible back ache.

Late in the head clerk's career, a time and motion expert visited Malawi and after several months' investigation concluded that the registers of incoming and outgoing mail served no useful purpose. He consequently recommended that they be abolished, and the Government accepted his recommendation. Thereafter, time and time again, the District Commissioner was embarrassed by not being able to trace correspondence and particularly by not being sure whether, or how, a letter had been answered. He spoke with the head clerk about this dilemma and was pleasantly surprised by the head clerk's ability after a few moments to tell him exactly where the letters in question had been filed and what the replies had been. As always, the District Commissioner was deeply impressed by the old man's astonishing memory, and on the day he retired he asked him to what he attributed his phenomenal powers of recall which seemed to have become enhanced in recent years. The head clerk smiled and beckoned to the DC to follow him into his office. There he carefully shut the door and quietly opened a locked cupboard from which he drew two large and heavy registers. He opened them gently and showed the DC how he had carefully copied, in immaculate copper plate handwriting, all the previous entries in both the incoming and outgoing mail registers, reaching back over many years, before they were destroyed. His was a wisdom which he shared with Sam Goldwyn who, when his secretary suggested that they should dispose of all out of date files, replied: 'A good idea, only be sure to make a copy of everything before getting rid of it.'

ooo ☺ ☻ ooo

THE CHIEF SECRETARY

Underneath runs the current of preoccupation, which is keeping one's nose clean at all times. This means that when things go wrong you have to pass the blame along the line, like pass-the-parcel, till the music stops.

Tom Stoppard.

Many unkind remarks were made, and stories told, about secretariat officers, particularly Chief Secretaries, by district officers who accused them, occasionally correctly, of never having travelled beyond such and such a point only a few miles from the secretariat, in Nyasaland's case that they had never been north of Liwonde on the Shire River. Not that district officers particularly wanted them to do so – and certainly not to their own districts. Let us take two such stories, at random, both about the same Chief Secretary.

I

It had long been the tradition that secretariat officers, no matter how junior, had been encouraged to give their own views and recommendations when forwarding papers 'up the chain' to their more senior colleagues. In the case of our Chief Secretary he had either not been given this encouragement or had 'adjusted' it as he rose up the ladder to occupy his present exalted position. It may be that he had reached that position at least in part by never having expressed his own opinion and consequently could never be contradicted by his seniors. And who could blame him, especially when his governor had very strong views of his own on most subjects and when it was not always possible to judge in advance precisely what those views might be? Therein lay the Chief Secretary's dilemma. He was a master of examining all aspects of a question and carefully weighing them in the delicate balance of his mind. Unable to gauge what opinion might best find favour with His Excellency, he would skilfully condense all the alternative courses of action into a precisely worded minute that ended, 'Your Excellency, We can do either A or B. I feel there is merit in both.'

The Governor, who looked for the facts and probably did not require any advice on action to be taken - indeed he was heard to say in private that as the chief executive he did not need a Chief Secretary – was content not to be guided by others, and he consequently tolerated the beautifully written and finely balanced minutes sent up to him by his Chief Secretary. None the less, very shortly before he retired, he decided to amuse himself at the Chief Secretary's expense. When next he received a minute, 'We can do either A or B. I feel there is merit in both', he sent it back, simply marking it in red ink, 'I agree.'

II

The story is told, too, that when the Chief Secretary died, after faithfully serving his country in the colonies for so many years, he went to heaven and on his arrival at the pearly gates St. Peter welcomed him most warmly, congratulated him on his CMG and explained that it was customary for newcomers to be placed in one or other of the domestic departments of heaven before moving on to more exalted and no doubt more appropriate responsibilities. He explained what these departments were and asked the Chief Secretary where he would like to work. The CS thought for a while – St. Peter thought rather a long while – and eventually said, 'The kitchen, please.' St. Peter smiled gently and said, 'Excellent. Now, let's start right away, shall we?' He led the way – floating rather than walking, to the Chief Secretary's relief - to the kitchen, sat him down in front of a huge pile of potatoes, and said, 'Now, I want you to sort these potatoes into two piles, one of large potatoes and the other of small potatoes. Is that all right?' The Chief Secretary meekly replied 'Yes.' St. Peter then said he had to go out for a while but when he came back he would call in to see how he was getting on. Several hours later, St. Peter returned, entered the kitchen and was most deeply distressed to find the CS sitting, head in his hands and crying bitterly, the pile of potatoes untouched in front of him. 'What on earth' – a nice touch since they were in heaven – he enquired 'is the matter?' Sobbing heavily and shaking his head in anguish, the Chief Secretary replied, 'Big ones, little ones, big ones, little ones. Decisions, decisions. I can't stand it!'

ooo ☺ ☻ ooo

He bellowed at me, the CS,
'How can you possibly make such mess?'
And my, how he laughed
when he picked up the draft,
and tore it to shreds, more or less.

THE MINISTER

But the privilege and the pleasure
that we treasure beyond measure
is to run little errands for the Ministers of State.
W S Gilbert.

I

During the Federation period in the early 1960s, one of the Nyasaland Cabinet Ministers, a rather short man, inspected a Local Court, where he found to his fury that on one of the walls there was a large portrait of the Federal prime minister, Sir Roy Welensky, a man greatly detested among Malawian politicians as the leader of an evil regime. When challenged, the terrified court clerk, instead of explaining that the portrait had been hanging unnoticed in its dark corner since long before he had arrived there, said the first thing that came into his head: he stammered that the portrait was there to show the difference between the evil Welensky and the universally admired and splendid Minister. When asked to explain, he said it was there to show to all and sundry that Welensky was a big man and the Minister was a small man. Quickly realizing that he was digging himself even more deeply into the mire, he added that he meant size in physical terms, certainly not quality, and it was clear to everyone that in political and intellectual quality the Minister was a giant and Welensky was but a dwarf. The Minister ordered that he be dismissed immediately, and he was led off in handcuffs.

The District Commissioner, who was present and had stood by quietly watching the proceedings, was naturally disturbed that politicians should think that they could dismiss public servants just as they pleased, but he felt that there was little he could do about it during a period when his instructions from on high were not to rock the political boat. None the less, he took the opportunity to check the court financial records, found several quid missing, and was able thereby to have the clerk prosecuted and convicted. In doing so he was able to re-establish the constitutional principle that Ministers do not dismiss public servants, and coincidentally to demonstrate the validity of the maxim which he was fond of quoting, that there are more ways of killing a cat than shoving a tin of condensed milk down its throat.

II

There was, too, the Minister who delivered a speech at a Local Court, drafted at his request by the District Commissioner, about the need for transparency in judicial proceedings. The Minister - who was known to have grave personal doubts about transparency in any matter - read the speech in English and it was interpreted into Chicewa. Freud in, I guess, heaven must have smiled through his beard as the Minister reached his resounding peroration which his interpreter translated with the words 'Justice must not be done but must seem to be done.'

III

And there was the Minister who sang the praises of an unusually cooperative and politically sympathetic European government officer by saying, 'He may have a white skin but he has a black heart. Indeed, he is not a pale-skin but a blackguard.'

ooo ☺ ☻ ooo

REGIMENTAL SERGEANT-MAJORS

By any criterion remarkable men.
Philip Mitchell.

In his memoirs, *African Afterthoughts*, written after he retired in 1952, Sir Philip Mitchell, who had been an Assistant Resident in Nyasaland from 1912 to 1915 and who became governor of Uganda, Fiji and Kenya, recalled the soldiers with whom he served in Nyasaland during the First World War:

'The fully trained African soldier, especially the warrant and non-commissioned officers … were by any criterion remarkable men … They were self-reliant, smart, efficient and wholly dependable … No one, in those days, would say bluntly that these African warrant officers were [the newly appointed subalterns'] superiors, but that was the fact; and they dealt with us, while they taught us our business, tactfully and sensibly, so that they were respected and obeyed … There were many striking personalities among these men. Sergeant-Major Nderemani, for instance, barely five feet tall, with a flaring cavalry moustache and a back straight as a ramrod; he had won the DCM at Gumburu in Somaliland in 1902 or 1903, when two British officers with him were awarded the Victoria Cross, for a joint act of great gallantry in saving wounded men … Colour-Sergeant Alfani, one of three brothers all of whom became Regimental Sergeant-Majors and were decorated, a man of fine and sensitive nature and a natural leader. Sergeants David and Furani, reservists; they too became sergeant-majors and earned decorations for gallantry; David was killed in action but Furani survived the war to be hall porter for me at Government House, Uganda. Magomero who was Sergeant-Major of the 1st Battalion when I was Adjutant, as gallant and loyal – and competent – a soldier as ever held his rank, and some higher.'

RSM BANDAWE

Regimental Sergeant-Major Bandawe was an Mtonga from the West Nyasa District. In 1895 he was sent by Alfred Sharpe with Corporal William Fletcher and a small unit of Sikh and Atonga soldiers to defend the Scottish missionaries at Chief Malemia's village near Domasi from attack by Chief Kawinga. With Fletcher he built a small fort known as Fletcher's Boma and successfully defended it against Kawinga's attacks. When their ammunition was running low, Bandawe suggested to Fletcher that they should charge the enemy, and they sallied forth firing their last volleys. At the sight of their gleaming bayonets, Kawinga's men turned and fled and were pursued for many miles by Bandawe with the Sikh and Atonga soldiers.

Later in 1895 Bandawe, having been promoted from Sergeant to RSM, was sent to the north of the country to help apprehend Mlozi bin Kazbadema. At first they could not find Mlozi but then, as Johnston related at the time, 'After the Sikhs and officers had given up searching Mlozi's house, Bandawe had remained behind feeling certain that there was some secret hiding place. After an interval during which he remained perfectly quiet he fancied he heard voices speaking underground. In the corner of the main room was a bedstead, and under the bed was an opening leading to an underground chamber. Crawling under the bed, Bandawe heard Mlozi asking, 'Who is there?' Mimicking the voice of a Swahili, he replied, 'It is I, Master' and descended into the underground chamber, where he found Mlozi being guarded by a man with a spear. Bandawe had no weapon with him but threw himself on the man and wrenched his spear from him which he then ran through his body. Turning to Mlozi he threatened to kill him at once unless he followed him without resistance. Mlozi, who was stupid with his wound, did so and he was safely brought to the camp [on a machila] by Bandawe.'

In later life, Johnston gave more details of Bandawe's capturing Mlozi. In this account Bandawe was called upon to explain to Johnston and Dr. Wordsworth Poole how Mlozi's injuries had come about: 'He had entered the town with the general rush of troops, but having been there before as a boy, he knew more or less the site of Mlozi's house. With a few armed Atonga he entered it very quietly. It seemed utterly deserted, but after a wait of about an hour, when the clamour of the invading forces had died down, his attention was aroused by some slight noise. He saw a large wooden shutter, which had been part of the floor, being pushed on one side, and a man's arm coming up to clutch at some support. With a shout to his few men he flung himself on the arm, pushed away the board, seized a throat and half strangled its owner, and with his five or six Atonga found himself in an underground chamber. Here on some kind of bed lay Mlozi, partly incapacitated by a gunshot wound. Bandawe in the sincerest accents made it clear that any resistance would be immediately followed by death, and presently he got Mlozi lifted up onto an upper floor, and so brought him out of the building and the town.'

Bandawe had been taught at Livingstonia Mission by Dr. Laws and he learned to play the organ there. He made the habit, after each successful military operation, of making his way to the nearest mission station with some of his men. He would sling his rifle on his back, sit down and play the organ or harmonium and sing hymns of triumph.

Johnston described him as 'invaluable as an intelligence officer, honest and trustworthy and unfalteringly brave.' He was awarded the Central Africa Medal in 1896, retired in 1899 and drew his government pension of £40 a year until he died in 1932.

RSM MAGOMERO, DCM

Regimental Sergeant-Major Magomero was a Henga from northern Nyasaland although he spent most of his life in the South. As a young man he enlisted in the Central African Rifles when it was raised in 1896, and served with it and its successor regiment, the King's African Rifles, for the next twenty-five years. During that time he rose to the rank of Regimental Sergeant-Major and was awarded the Distinguished Conduct Medal for courage in battle. He retired in 1921 and immediately enlisted in the Nyasaland Police, which was being reorganized on semi-military lines in that year. He served with the Police until 1939, retiring as Force Sergeant-Major just before the Second World War. When war was declared he immediately re-enlisted in the KAR even though he must have been over 60 years of age, and served with them until 1945. In 1952, as nationalist political activity increased, the Government raised the Police Mobile Force - the riot squad - as a rapid reaction unit to deal with civil disturbance. The first in the line to join the PMF was Magomero, and he served with them for a short time before he sought further employment, this time with the Land Settlement Department at Chingale where the officer in charge described him: 'Ramrod straight and impeccably turned out in a starched khaki bush jacket and shorts, puttees and polished boots, Sam Browne belt, bush hat emblazoned with the letters 'RSM' and a row of medals long enough to make Goering envious.' At this time he had next to no money, and he needed employment, for in the days of his service, retirement carried a gratuity and not a pension, and though he had earned three gratuities, all had long been eaten up in looking after his relatives, and he was destitute. He was taken on at Chingale, where he stayed for two years, as supernumerary Head Messenger. He had no particular duties, but his outstanding presence, prestige and reputation added much to the local scene.

RSM AIBU CHIKWENGA, BEM

Regimental Sergeant-Major Aibu Chikwenga, BEM, formerly of the King's African Rifles, started to write his autobiography in the early 1960s, partly in Chichewa and partly in Chiyao, and completed it in June 1970. He died a few years later. Aibu felt fairly certain that he was born in 1891, but believes that it is possible that he was born earlier than this. The following extract covers his period of service in the Army.

'One day in the middle of 1914 the Governor, Sir Alfred Sharpe, knowing that I had travelled in Tanganyika and knew the road well, sent me to the house of General Llewellyn, the officer commanding the armed forces of the country, so that I could help him get to Karonga and then to Tanganyika. General Llewellyn was a well-mannered man and was quite kind, but because we could not understand his language, English, he used to shout at us and repeat himself to make sure that we understood what he was saying, and this gave him the appearance of being a fierce man. We started our journey and had only been gone two weeks when war broke out between Britain and Germany, so we hurried back to Zomba, and I left the employment of General Llewellyn and started to work, as a domestic servant, for Mr. Tucker.

By this time my father was working as a watchman for Mr.Togodo who lived near Mpalanganga, seven miles from Zomba on the Blantyre road. One night early in 1915 he heard some people on the road saying that the Alomwe were killing the white people at Chiradzulu - this was the John Chilembwe Rising - so my father knocked loudly at the door of Mr. Togodo's bedroom, and they took him to Zomba for safety. At that time we saw soldiers moving everywhere, and no one was allowed to carry a knife or other weapon. The Alomwe, who used to file their teeth, used to walk around with their mouth closed so that no one would know they were Alomwe, so as to keep out of trouble.

NYASALAND-MALAWI ANECDOTES

As soon as the First World War started the British began to recruit people in this country to join the Army and to fight against the Germans. My brother-in-law, Amusa Maonga, joined the Army and went away to Kenya, and I decided to do the same. On 26th June 1916, in the morning, I prepared Mr. Tucker's breakfast, and whilst he was eating it I went to the Army and enrolled as a soldier. The KAR officials gave me a uniform to wear and handed me a letter to give to my employer saying that I had enlisted as a soldier. I went to Mr. Tucker with the letter and he saw me wearing my khaki uniform. When he had read the letter he looked at me and said, "As it is your desire to join the Army, it is all right. Here is your pay for this month." At the Army camp in Zomba we were issued with rifles and bayonets and were taught how to fight. We were treated very well and I enjoyed myself. I particularly liked the target practice. I joined the Army for the sake of helping my government which was protecting us from the Germans.

In the year 1917 I was sent to Lindi in Tanganyika to fight. I also went to Chipoya, where there was a great battle against the Germans. Many people, including my brother Amini and my brother-in-law Amusa, were killed in this dreadful battle. From Nairobi we travelled to Lindi by steam train, and here we fought hard and captured two towns. After this we went to Masasa where we fought a battle for eight days and nights. Again at Mingoyi we had another great battle, and our main reason for fighting here was that at Mingoyi there were many mango trees and much sugar cane which we wanted to obtain because we were very hungry. Many soldiers on both sides were killed, and I particularly recall the bravery of one South African officer who fired a bren gun and killed many of the enemy. He was shot in the arm but he dressed the wound himself and continued to advance, firing his bren gun until he was shot in the leg. Then our great leader, General Platten, went and took him away and told him to rest.

In 1918 I went to Mpula in Portuguese East Africa, then to Lipawa and then to Malokotela. We ended the war in November 1918 at 11.00 a.m. After the war there was a great outbreak of influenza and many people died. When those of us who survived got better we went to Lindi where we had a big celebration which we called a coronation.

In 1919 the KAR soldiers returning from the war arrived in Limbe and we all camped at the place where the Roman Catholic cathedral now is. We handed in all our weapons but were allowed to keep some of our uniforms and our blankets, and we were given a gratuity. I was awarded two medals during the war.

Only a year later, however, I was asked to go back into the Army, and I re-enlisted on 28th December 1920 at Zomba. I spent nine years in the Army at that time, and travelled to Tabora, Kigoma, Zanzibar and Monga. I was discharged on 27th December 1929. The very next day I began work as a domestic servant with Mr. Mallet, whom I had known since we were at Tabora together in the Army. I continued this domestic work until the Second World War started.

On 18th October 1940 Mr. Mallet and I joined the Army together again, and two weeks later I was made a Corporal. I joined the 1st and 2nd KAR and was sent to Ekwendeni. It was during the Second World War that I received much promotion: Sergeant on 18th November 1940; Company Sergeant-Major on 1st January 1941; and Regimental Sergeant-Major on 16th July 1942. All these promotions were conferred upon me because of my bravery. I also travelled a great deal: in Somaliland and Abyssinia; to Jiputi, Nairobi and Jinja - all with the 2nd Battalion of the King's African Rifles. In 1947 I was awarded the British Empire Medal.

The Second World War was very different from the First, because, in the First, from start to finish we had to travel on foot; there were no cars and no aeroplanes (except one used for carrying mail), and no shoes and no tea. But the Second World War, although it was tiresome, it was interesting: every morning we started the day with a cup of tea; we did all our long-distance travelling in vehicles; when we were fighting in difficult places, there were aeroplanes to assist us by coming in and dropping bombs; sometimes we travelled in aeroplanes; furthermore, we had shoes to wear.

I stayed in the Army after the War, and in 1951 my battalion went to Southern Rhodesia with other battalions to have a great competition, especially in rifle-firing. I got the highest marks in my battalion, and my battalion beat all the others and came first. The Governor of Southern Rhodesia and the most senior officer in the Central and East Africa armed forces, made me stand up before all the people, and the Governor said, 'This is the man who has won the competition which we have been watching', and all the people clapped their hands in happiness and praise. After we left the camp in Rhodesia, it was burned down.

I was finally discharged from the Army at Zomba on 7th January 1952, when I had completed twenty-three years and thirty-six days of service in the Army.'

RSM MWAFULI, MSM

On 4 August 1923 *The Nyasaland Times* published the obituary of Regimental Sergeant-Major Mwafuli:

'We regret to announce that Regimental Sergeant-Major Mwafuli, 1st King's African Rifles, died at Zomba on the 29th July 1923, from pneumonia.

The deceased Warrant Officer had 23 years' service and served in the following countries: Somaliland 1902-1904; Somaliland 1909-1910; Jubaland, 1912-1913; Zanzibar 1913-1914; German East Africa 1916-1918. He was in possession of the following medals; Ashanti, Somaliland, 1914-1918, British Victory, Meritorious Service, and Long Service and Good Conduct.

By his untimely and much regretted death the 1st King's African Rifles are deprived of an efficient Warrant Officer. He is greatly missed by Officers, Non-Commissioned Officers and men alike, and his place will be hard to fill.

His funeral was most impressive and took place with full military honours at Liwambwe village on 31 July. It was attended by the Colonel, Adjutant and all the available Officers. The Drums of the Battalion and 100 Rank and File under the command of Captain I B Moir, MC, also took part and every mark of respect and esteem was paid by all to the late distinguished Warrant Officer.'

RSM ALI KIONGWE

On 11 November 1890, Sir Harry Johnston read a paper at the Royal Geographical Society in London. In it he paid tribute to his 'invaluable Swahili headman', Ali Kiongwe, who a few years later became Regimental Sergeant-Major of Johnston's early army in British Central Africa. Johnston had employed him the previous year in Zanzibar, at the beginning of his journey, at the request of the Foreign Office, to 'report fully on the critical situation which had arisen through the war with the Arabs on Lake Nyassa, and, if possible, to bring such war to an end by negotiation with the Arabs.' Kiongwe accompanied him throughout this journey. He lost his sight in later years and died in about 1912.

'When a lad of 14 or 15 he made a remarkable journey on his own account, accompanying an Arab caravan to Lake Nyassa and the river Loangwa, learning on this occasion, and retaining ever afterwards in his memory, the leading African dialects spoken in this region. Then, on his return to Zanzibar, he joined Stanley's expedition of 1875, and accompanied Stanley throughout the whole of that memorable journey across the continent, when the course of the Congo was first made known to geography. When Stanley returned to the Congo Kiongwe immediately rejoined him, and worked for three years more on the Congo, where I first made his acquaintance. When I met him again at Zanzibar, in 1884, I made him the headman of my Kilimanjaro expedition, where, in a hundred instances, he displayed the bravery, astuteness, and fertility of resource which are so characteristic of the good Swahili. After this he did excellent work for the Universities' Mission in Usambara. Then he joined Count Teleki's expedition, and with this daring Hungarian explorer he made that remarkable journey through Masailand which resulted in the discovery of Lake Samburu.

After this, at my recommendation, he was chosen to be the headman of the expedition led into Masailand by the late Honourable Guy Dawnay, whose unfortunate death by a buffalo, all who have known him will never cease to deplore. After his master's death Kiongwe, with great pluck and cunning, managed to recover from the Masai, who had robbed the dead body, the watch and rings which Mr. Dawnay wore at the time of his death. For this and other services rendered in connection with this sad event, the relations of the late Mr. Dawnay have presented Kiongwe with a very handsome watch and chain as a mark of their esteem. After a short rest Kiongwe joined me again on this last expedition, and has remained in my service ever since. I can not sufficiently praise his honesty, pluck, and devotion.'

RSM JACK ARCHER, MBE, DCM

Jack Archer was born into a modest yeoman farming family in Essex on the first day of 1871. He left school at the age of twelve and entered the wine and spirit trade in London. Preferring a career that would enable him to see the world, he joined the Rifle Brigade on his eighteenth birthday. Most of his first seven years in the army was spent in Ireland, where he progressed rapidly through the ranks to become a Colour Sergeant at the age of 27. A great deal of his time in Ireland was devoted to athletics, in which he excelled, winning many medals, trophies and prizes, and becoming Champion of the Army. He was also a successful boxer and a remarkable rifle marksman.

His first period of overseas active service was as Armourer Sergeant with the Mounted Infantry in the Mashonaland Campaign of 1896-7. A year later he was a member of Kitchener's Nile Expedition and fought at the Battle of Omdurman, and this was followed by service in Malta and Crete. Then in 1899 he moved with his battalion to South Africa, arriving in Ladysmith on the eve of the siege. He was engaged in a good deal of fighting in South Africa, and particularly distinguished himself at the Battle of Surprise Hill, for which he was awarded the DCM. After a period in Egypt and the Sudan from 1902 to 1905, he was posted to India. In 1908 he was seconded as Regimental Sergeant-Major of the First Battalion of the King's African Rifles in Nyasaland and served with them in Somaliland in

1908 and 1909. He stayed in Nyasaland until the outbreak of the First World War in 1914, when he rejoined his parent regiment and went to France with the British Expeditionary Force. Only three weeks after war was declared, during the retreat from Mons, he was very seriously wounded in the thigh and taken prisoner. He spent the remainder of the war in a prison camp, and was thereby deprived of the commission he had been offered, and accepted, on the outbreak of the war.

At the end of the war he left the army and was appointed to the Nyasaland Civil Service as Superintendent of the Central Prison, Lunatic Asylum and Leprosarium, a position he held for twenty years until retiring in 1939. During this period he introduced a number of progressive reforms into the management of the Central Prison and the treatment of the prisoners, and was awarded the MBE in recognition of these services. He led a very active social life, playing football, cricket and hockey for Zomba, and particularly excelling at competitive rifle shooting. In this last sport he shot regularly for the Nyasaland team at Bisley and, at home, won all the major shooting trophies, in nearly all cases several years running. He was an active member of the Freemasons' Lodge David Livingstone, having previously been a member of the craft in Egypt and India.

When war was declared in 1939, though recently retired from the Civil Service, and aged 68, he rejoined the KAR and was commissioned. His war service was entirely in Nyasaland and was mainly concerned with recruit training and depot command.

He retired again in 1947, with 38 years' army service and a total 58 years' crown service behind him. He spent the remainder of his life at Naiwale Estate, where he and his family now lived, ten miles south of Zomba. He died in 1954, aged 83, and was buried in the Zomba Cemetery. His 16 campaign and other medals are on display at the Royal Green Jackets' Museum, Winchester, a permanent tribute to one who, as the inscription on his gravestone recalls, was indeed 'A Man Among Men'.

CONTEMPT

In 1964 there were separate army mutinies in Zambia, Uganda and Tanzania. When the last of these occurred the Commanding Officer of the Malawi Army, who happened to be in East Africa, returned immediately to Malawi by air. When he arrived in Zomba he discovered – as he had both hoped and expected – that all was well and there were no signs of his men being other than their usual steady selves.

The following day, early in the morning, the Brigadier had the whole regiment formally paraded and he gave them a full account of what had happened in East Africa. His speech was also designed as a morale booster.

When he had finished speaking he turned to the Regimental Sergeant-Major and said 'Carry on, Sar'nt Major.' The RSM, his highly polished pace stick under his arm, his back like a ramrod, his buttons, badges and medals gleaming in the bright sunlight, came to attention with a parade ground shattering stamp of his gleaming boots, saluted smartly with a mighty sweep of his arm and roared so that none could miss what he was saying. He thanked the Brigadier for his words and proceeded: 'Sah! We have always considered the East African soldiers our brothers in arms, but,' and here his voice, a voice strengthened with years of barking parade ground instructions, momentarily quivered, not through timidity but through anger and disgust, 'but today, Sah, they have shown themselves to be just garden boys.' The contempt in his voice and the expression of disdain on his face were awesome as he repeated with a scornful sneer, 'Just garden boys, Sah!

ooo ☺ ☻ ooo

THE MOBILE CINEMA

Field officers in the 1940s and 1950s sometimes took with them on *ulendo*, a mobile cinema, the electricity coming from a generator carried on a lorry and the films being provided by either the Central Office of Information or the British Council. The performances were after dark since they were done in the open air. Their purpose was to educate and to entertain.

I

At the Agricultural Department's request, a film was shown to demonstrate the folly of poor cultivation practices and the rewards to be gained by good practice. The film had two reels.

The first showed a rather clownish village farmer cultivating his maize on steeply sloping land without forming the soil into contour ridges and without using any manure or fertilizer. He did scarcely any work and spent most of the day idly drinking beer on the *khonde* of his house, exchanging tales with his equally lethargic male neighbours. Occasionally, once the rains really started in earnest, he roused himself on one elbow to tell his wife to go outside and drop a few maize seeds into the loose soil nearby. A few months later, as the maize ripened and dried, he was still drinking on the *khonde* as he sent his obliging and much over-worked wife to gather the cobs and place them in the family *nkhokwe*. Since his garden was on virgin land, his crop for the first year was excellent. The cobs were so plump and so numerous that he could not count them. They were so numerous in fact that he could spare an unusual amount for the brewing - by his wife again – of a drum or two of beer. The cinema farmer was a splendid comic, performing his part with the most amusing of antics. The audience loved it and the Agricultural Officer who was showing the film was delighted because the punch line, the point at which entertainment brutally gave way to education, came in the second reel. 'You may laugh now', he mused, 'but wait till you see the second half.'

In this next reel the productivity of the first year would give way in subsequent years to appalling poverty. Heavy rain would wash away the top soil into raging streams of brown-red mud. The farmer would soon find himself, or rather his poor wife, trying to plant the few seeds they now had on almost bare rock. He would even have to get off the *khonde* and help her – he might just as well, he would think in his despair, because there was no longer any beer to drink. Their children would become thinner and thinner and more and more sickly and his wife would become increasingly exhausted. The lesson would be clear for all to behold; no one could miss it. Or so the Agricultural Officer thought. As the audience settled down ready to see the sequel, still laughing excitedly and mimicking the antics of the cinema farmer they had just seen on the screen, the cinema operator came up to him and whispered in his ear, '*Bwana*, we've forgotten to bring the second reel.'

II

Without doubt, the most popular films were those of Charlie Chaplin. His antics and extraordinary acting ability delighted packed village audiences. Both adults and children roared with laughter, screeched with delight, giggled incessantly and for days after a show would be seen mimicking the clowning of their beloved 'Charlie Chuplink'. They clamoured noisily and excitedly for repeat performances and whole evenings could pass with up to half a dozen showings, one after the other until the fuel for the generator began to run low. Charlie did more to win the hearts and minds of village Africa than any Western politician could possibly have done – thank heavens!

III

Film shows in the villages were immensely popular and the audiences would sit enthralled, often irrespective of what was actually being portrayed on the screen. It would take a quite extraordinary happening to divert them from watching. There was, however, an occasion when there was such a diversion. The film being shown was Trooping the Colour on Horse Guards Parade in London. Now, it is readily accepted that this annual spectacle lost much of its attraction when, as was the case in the 1940s and 1950s, the film was black and white and not in Glorious Technicolor, but this was not a factor in the audience's attention being diverted. No. The film was being taken round the district by a District Commissioner of the old school, a man of unshakeable patriotism, one devoted to the British Empire and a stickler for propriety. While the film was being shown he was sitting alone and eating his dinner of groundnut soup, curried chicken and mango fool just outside his tent. Gradually, the audience left the space where the film was being shown and silently crept towards the DC's tent. They crouched down in the grass a little distance from the tent and watched, enthralled and puzzled to start with but, as time passed, with more and more amusement until they could no longer contain their mirth in silence. Their outburst of unrestrainable laughter reached the replete DC's ear as, having just started a cigar and about to take a sip of his port, the National Anthem was played for the fifth time at the Trooping the Colour, and for the fifth time this stalwart of imperialism leapt to his feet, stood rigidly to attention and saluted smartly.

ooo ☺ ☻ ooo

JAILOS CHINGOTA

The autobiography of Jailos Chingota, originally written in Chicewa in the 1960s, deals with the history of his own people and of himself, but in doing so, since he worked with and knew many of the very early Europeans in British Central Africa, it also deals with their history. He came into contact, often quite close contact, with a remarkable number of these early white visitors, both settlers and officials from many government departments. It is an account of the closing years of the nineteenth and the opening years of the twentieth centuries, an account - whatever its possible inaccuracies and the spelling of names - as those formative years were experienced and understood by an acutely observant and perceptive Malawian blessed with an unusually fine memory.

Jailos became a much travelled man. Between 1899 and 1905, while working on the surveys of Nyasaland's international boundaries with Mozambique, German East Africa and Northern Rhodesia, he travelled around the whole of the country, from Lulwe in the very south of the country to Chitipa in the very north; from Mchinji in the west to Madziabango in the east; along the whole of Lake Malawi's western coast line and the length of the Shire River. There was scarcely a district headquarters that he did not visit. His detailed accounts of these surveys and of the subsequent building of many major roads are unique.

He was a man with exceptional leadership qualities, whether as overseer goatherd boy, or labour roll checker, or estate overseer, or assistant tax collector, or survey capitao, or general supervisor, or undertaking the Indian surveyors' work when they were exhausted, or Road Roller Driver Grade One, which was his rank when he retired from the civil service. He was, too, a man of unusual wisdom and shrewdness – who but such a man would have habitually carried salt in the pockets of his 'long short trousers' or could locate water by listening to the croaking of frogs?

His autobiography covers the years up to 1915. When asked what he did after 1915 he dismissed it as uninteresting and unimportant. In fact, he continued to work for the Public Works Department until retiring on 1 April 1936 after 40 years' service. He was awarded the Certificate of Honour in 1935 and became an Assessor at Chief Chikowi's Court in 1937. He rejoined the Public Works Department in 1945, working in Zomba Township, and in 1949 became the Works Supervisor for the Zomba Town Council, which post he occupied until well into the 1960s by which time he must have been in at least his mid eighties. He died in the early 1970s.

'When members of the Yao tribe were attacked by the Ngoni in their homeland, a number of chiefs and their followers left and emigrated first to the Mangoche Hill area and then to Makongwe near Chikala Hill. Later there were further movements and Msonde, my grandfather, went to Ulongwe where, after a gift of a blanket and cloth had been given by the Yao Chief Kapeni to the Mang'anja headman Sanyala, he was allowed to settle. The senior Mang'anja Chiefs Kankhomba and M'bona, however, objected to Yao immigration and despite being given presents they murdered Kapeni's senior wife when she was paying them a courtesy visit. This murder sparked off retaliations in which the Yaos marched over the whole area from Chiradzulu to Mpatamanga, destroying the Mang'anja. While at Kanjedza my mother's father was shot by a Mang'anja arrow and I had the bow, from which it was fired, in my possession until 1932 when I mislaid it.

It was about this time that David Livingstone first arrived in the country and shortly the Yao chiefs became firmly settled, Kapeni at Soche, Matope at Ndirande, Lundu at Mpemba, Somba south of Soche, Mpama at Chiradzulu, Njowe at Linjisi and Chingota, my father, at Chichiri. Their peace was disturbed first by a battle which they fought against the Makololo between Ntonda Hill and Mbame stream, and then by the Angoni. Njowe, who had settled at Linjisi, had chased away Sanyala who later assisted the

Angoni in a big battle at Chimvuu. Njowe was killed and his people fled towards Blantyre where the Yao, hearing the fearful news, climbed Ndirande mountain and lived there for a while.

While they were living on Ndirande a European arrived on the scene, Henry Henderson, who was known to the Yao as 'Ntebe'. After some minor initial difficulties, Chief Kapeni sent my father, Chingota, to help Henderson to find a place to establish a Mission. Together they visited Ndirande, Limbe, Chigumula and Soche but no place suited the European until having crossed the Mudi River they reached Kalimeje's village. A short while after this Henderson collected his friends from the Zambezi and they all settled at Kalimeje's and built the Blantyre Mission.

Among the Europeans who then came to Blantyre were Mr. Macdonald, - known as 'Masom'mwamba'; Frederick Moir known as 'Chindebvu'; John Moir known as 'Mandala'; John Buchanan known as 'Makanani'; and Mr. Fenwick. Once, when Angoni warriors were encamped near my father's village, John Moir rode out on a white horse to the Angoni camp. The white horse so frightened the warriors that they moved away quickly from Blantyre and went to Malabvi where the Yao people rolled trees and boulders upon then until they dispersed.

On another occasion a man, Solomanje, and two of his friends, murdered Solomanje's wife because she was suspected of misbehaving herself at a dance. Mr. Macdonald arrested all three culprits but the two friends escaped. Solomanje, however, was shot for his misdeeds and as a result Mr. Macdonald was recalled to Scotland and John Buchanan set himself up as a private coffee planter. Mr. Fenwick also got himself into trouble; when he left the mission he engaged in trade and, following a quarrel, killed Chief Chiputula in Chikwawa, and was himself killed by the chief's followers on an island in the Shire river. Chiputula was succeeded by his son, Chikuse, who engaged in the mischief of stealing goods from European boats on the river. The senior Makololo chief, Kasisi, was annoyed by these activities and ordered the execution of Chikuse. As he was being shot Chikuse prophesied Kasisi's death by saying, 'Tell my father, Chief Kasisi, to eat quickly for soon he will follow me.' Kasisi died within a few days, suffering from a swelling in the gullet. Chikuse was succeeded by his Uncle, Mlauli, who had been David Livingstone's house boy, was able to speak English and was educated at Blantyre Mission. Mlauli, like his predecessor, began to interfere with goods being carried on the river and so annoyed was John Moir that he asked the Portuguese to attack Mlauli. The Portuguese agreed and sent troops upriver between Chiromo and Chikwawa. Mlauli first ran away to Cholo and then to Neno where his family now lives.

The Moir brothers, Monteith Fotheringham (known as 'Follium Mwantisi') and his young brother Dr. Fotheringham, lived on very good terms with their neighbour, my father. My brother, Sani, and two others went with John Moir to Quelimane and helped to assemble the steamer 'Packet' which they then brought up to Chikwawa. So impressed were the people with this great achievement that the three helpers marked the occasion by changing their names, one calling himself ever thereafter 'Packet'. John Moir also travelled to Karonga and purchased cattle, returning with Ankhonde cattlemen who were known to us as 'Asokiri' because their traditional greeting was 'sokiri'.

By this time other Europeans had come to the country: Mr. Lindsay was called 'Manjanja' because he walked as if he had the palsy; Mr. Samuel was nicknamed 'Kamfwamba' because he had the gait of a kidnapper; Mr. Beaton was at Chinde, Mr. Macdonald at Chiromo; Mr. Virtue at Chikwawa, Mr. Nicholas at Matope; Mr. Chamberlain at Fort Johnston and the Fotheringham brothers at Karonga. All these people were the agents of the African Lakes Corporation which everyone knew as 'Mandala' after John Moir who was the manager and who wore spectacles, 'mandala'.

My father's people helped Mr. Moir to carry the steel plates from Chikwawa to Mphimbi to construct the new vessel 'Monteith'. They were each paid two yards of white calico from Chikwawa to Blantyre and four yards from Blantyre to Mphimbi. Then the 'Domira' was also constructed for sailing on the Lake.

Frederick Moir, who was a very accomplished elephant hunter, had a number of unfortunate misunderstandings with Chief Makanjira which resulted in a war. Mr. 'Kirra' was wounded and John Buchanan went to see Chief Makanjira. The chief seized both John Buchanan and his servant and, laying the latter across the knees of the former, he cut off the boy's head. Then Chief Makanjira sent John Buchanan away almost naked. After another war at Chikala against Kawinga Mr. Buchanan began his trip home to Scotland but unfortunately he died at Chinde on the way.

Mlozi, who lived on the Rukuru river, being jealous of Europeans who were collecting ivory in his area, launched an attack against Monteith Fotheringham at Karonga. Many of my father's people accompanied the Europeans who went to fight against Mlozi. In an attack on Mlozi's subordinate, Phwandaphwanda, two white men, called 'Ligogogo' and 'Liundi', were killed. Frederick Moir was wounded in the arm when he and the Yao were surrounding Mlozi's stockade. Although Frederick Moir went home to Scotland and did not return until the end of the First World War, John Moir and others fought and conquered Mlozi in 1891. Mlozi was hanged at Karonga for his misdeeds.

My first job was that of plate washer to John Moir, *Bwana* Mandala, and it was on the verandah of his house that I received my first lessons. Classes were taken in the afternoon by Henry Cowen Kapitao who was sent by Dr. Clement Scott. Henry had been the slave of Chief Masangano and had been educated in Scotland. By attending these classes I reached the 'Infant Reader' standard. I then became a cook for Mr. Moir but there were difficulties in my village where the elders objected to my not having been initiated. I felt ashamed because although I had refused to be initiated I had great respect for those who objected to my refusal and in addition until a chief's son was initiated many others could not be initiated. At last I agreed and with sixty others I spent six months learning the customs, manners and habits of my people, learned respect for my elders, and correct behaviour when on visits. While I was at the initiation course, my father, Chief Chingota, took some ivory to Chiwambo (Quelimane) to exchange for cloth, both spotted and unspotted, since this type of cloth was out of stock at Mandala. This cloth was a gift to me at the end of my initiation, the ceremonial dance of which was attended by Europeans from both Mandala and the Mission.

I had a five day rest after my initiation and then returned to work. Later I entered Standard III at the Mission where I was appointed overseer goatherd boy by the Mission capitao, Andy. I did not get on well with the goat boys and decided to leave. Despite the persuasion of the missionary-in-charge, the Reverend Smith, I refused to return and instead began teaching my relatives at home the lessons I had learned.

One day, as I was walking to Mandala, I met Mr. Cameron, Agricultural Officer, who asked me if I would work for him, helping him check his daily labour roll. I accepted and enjoyed my work. When Mr. John Burnett, who looked after Makoka Estate, died and became the first person buried in Zomba cemetery, I was asked by Mr. Gibbs, the Mandala manager, to take over the running of Makoka Estate. Mr. Gibbs was a great friend of all the Africans; he had succeeded Monteith Fotheringham who had taken over the management of the African Lakes Corporation from John Moir. I spent eighteen months at Makoka and then asked to be sent back to Blantyre. Mr. Gibbs, however, wanted me to go and look after Naboma Estate in Cholo where the European Manager had recently died. I did not want to go to Naboma because there were many lions there. Mr. Gibbs became angry with me and dismissed me. On my way home I was asked by Mr. James 'Mikell', the workshop manager at Mandala, if I would work for him. I agreed and one of my tasks was to help build the first Mandala store at Zomba in 1896.

When Mr. 'Mikell' went home on leave in 1897, I was loaned to his friend, Mr. Thomas I. Binnie who had formerly been a surveyor with the African Lakes Corporation but joined Government and had been given the job of opening up the Chikwawa road. Having finished that road we made the Matope road from Blantyre to Matope. All the time I was learning a great deal about road construction, the use of explosives, measuring, making corners and paying the labourers in cloth.

When the Chief Surveyor's Office was moved from Blantyre to Zomba in 1893 I went with the Chief Surveyor, Mr. William Anderson, and the Indian Surveyors, Mohamed Ali Khan, Jumali Din, Ramji, Taja and Jandika. One of our first tasks in Zomba was to construct the 'Masongola' Road up to the Old Residency. We also did surveying of land at Mlanje and Chinde but my most interesting job was helping to survey the international boundary between Nyasaland and Mozambique. This survey involved long journeys and my memory of it is very clear even to-day.

The reason for requiring the survey of the international border was that two Europeans, Mr. Sanderson and Mr. Walker, who were planters, went into Portuguese territory, to the area of Chief Mkwamba, to recruit labourers. They were unfortunately severely handled by the Portuguese Africans but managed to escape with their lives. Sir Alfred Sharpe, the Governor of Nyasaland, considered that the time had come for the boundary to be properly surveyed and demarcated. In 1899, therefore, a Boundary Committee was set up and consisted of Mr. Cunningham (Secretary) and Mr. Binnie (Surveyor) on behalf of the British, and Captains Blanco, Flossi, and Court on behalf of the Portuguese. Two Indians, Jumali Din and Jandika accompanied the Committee. I was Mr. Binnie's survey capitao.

We journeyed over to Mlanje and where the Ruo River leaves Mlanje Mountain we erected our first beacon; our second was on Mauzi. In view of the unsettled state of the country at that time, twelve soldiers who were normally stationed at Fort Lister were attached to the British party for protection purposes. The Portuguese officers also had a unit of military men at their disposal.

After erecting the first two beacons I was sent back to Zomba to erect survey beacons on Namikango, Mpyupyu and Sakata Hills and to collect food for the survey party. My return journey from Zomba was via Chikala Hill and Madziabango in which latter area we found the villages deserted because of internal strife. A company of King's African Rifles soldiers went ahead of me to accompany our survey team on their journeys. I eventually found the survey party at Mchimadzi.

Leaving Mr. Cunningham to look after the camp, Mr. Binnie and I took a journey by boat to Tongwe Island in Lake Chilwa. We found many people swimming across the Lake to Chikala to avoid oppression in Mozambique. Having surveyed on Tongwe Island we returned to Mchimadzi to find that our Indian surveyors had lost themselves in the bush. They were missing for three days before they returned, hungry and exhausted. As a result they had to return to Zomba and I was promoted to undertake their work.

When we erected beacon No.8 on the Konekone stream we found that the whole of Lake Chilwa fell in the British sphere. We travelled north camping at Madziabango, Chief Chikweo's village and Namalamba. While at Namalamba Mr. Cunningham left us since he was being transferred to Zanzibar, and his place was taken by Mr. Swan who had formerly been at Kota Kota.

We travelled north again with Mr. Swan and slept at the Portuguese fort at Kwitande. We wanted to travel eastwards to the Lujenda River but the people of Chief Mataka were hostile to us. We erected Beacon No.11 at Msimbiti where the half company of the King's African Rifles left us and returned to Zomba, and then we went on to Mgwalangwa Hill and Ndumundu Hill. I was very pleased to reach Ndumundu because I had been told that my parents had lived there before they emigrated to the Blantyre area. Soon we reached Mangoche Hill and were well received by the King's African Rifles soldiers garrisoned there. The remaining half company of soldiers who had so far accompanied us left us here and returned to Zomba. We were out of the dangerous country. After Mangoche we stayed at Chief Namwera's village where I met more of my relatives who had not followed my father when he went south to Blantyre. Two of my relatives, Nkwanda and Nasolo, accompanied us because they were well acquainted with the country roundabout. They helped us a great deal in avoiding a raiding party of Chief Mataka warriors at Makunganya's village. They also led us on to Lusyeti Hill where we placed beacon No.12, and to the Mlinete stream where we erected beacon No.13.

A little later we reached Fort Maguire where Dr. Figgins ordered his Sikh soldiers to fire 25 rounds to welcome us. So surprised was the local Chief Matola to hear the gunfire that, thinking Makanjila had attacked the *boma*, he and his people rushed quickly to Dr. Figgins's aid. For his faithful and prompt, if unnecessary, action Chief Matola was given 100 yards of cloth by Dr. Figgins.

After a few days' rest at the *boma* we went on, camped at the Msinje stream, crossed the Dwangwa river and placed beacon No. 14 on the Lupichi stream. We again tried to get to the Lujenda country but having crossed the upper Dwangwa we were once more turned back by hostile followers of Mataka. From Fort Maguire we took the 'Guendolen' to Fort Johnston where we were received by Mr. Ockenden, the District Commissioner.

Our survey of the south-eastern boundary of Nyasaland was completed but we carried on surveying in the Fort Johnston District. We surveyed from Mauni and Kongwe Hills and when we reached the Msipe River, the boundary of the Fort Johnston and Dedza Districts, Mr. Ockenden took his leave of us. Here our party split into two, Mr. Swan going to Chief

Kachindamoto's area whilst Mr. Binnie and I went on to Monkey Bay and then to Cape Maclear, where we stayed at the Church of Scotland Mission. Mr. Binnie was unwell here and we returned to meet Mr. Swan at Ntakataka in Chief Kachindamoto's area. We then all travelled together to Dedza *boma* where we met Mr. Godrick, who was called 'Chinkhondo' by the Africans. The District Commissioner explained to us that Chief Kachindamoto, having been arrested on a charge of murder, had committed suicide with a knife in the jail. The knife had been given to the chief by his wife at his request for the purpose of paring his nails.

Having surveyed in Dedza District we proceeded on to the Lilongwe District, crossing the Diampwe River and climbing Ngala-ya-pakamwa, Ngala-ya-maso and Mbuzinyama Hills. We then crossed the upper Bua River and surveyed many of the hills around Fort Manning, including Msilanyama on the Mozambique border.

While we were proceeding to Domwe Hill the Europeans went in advance of the carriers who unfortunately lost their way. The *bwanas*, therefore, found themselves without food. However, I was able to assist them and, begging eggs from Chief Kachere which I seasoned with salt which I habitually carried in the pockets of my long short trousers whilst on journeys, and roasting pounded maize sweetened with honey I was able to provide a meal of eggs and 'coffee' for both dinner and breakfast. They slept on their machilas and the carriers arrived at about 9.00 a.m. the next morning.

Having erected beacons on Domwe and Dedza Mountains we all went on to Fort Mlangeni where we met Captain Stockes. Here, at the instruction of my officers, I warned Chief Namulangeni not to move his village or he would find himself illegally in Portuguese Territory. I spent a whole week in January 1900 giving this advice and explaining the matter to the people. By this time it had become too wet to survey properly so we returned to Zomba, calling in on Mr. Yule the District Commissioner at Fort Liwonde and at Likwenu on our way. Sir Alfred Sharpe received the surveyors and showed much interest in the boundary map. The Portuguese officers then took their leave, having arranged to continue the boundary survey after the rains.

When Mr. Binnie went home to England on leave, arrangements were made for me to accompany him but I was unable to do so because my first born child died. Mr. Binnie returned to Nyasaland in August 1900, and in the September the Portuguese officers, with the exception of Captain Court, arrived to resume the boundary survey. We left Zomba and arriving at Fort Liwonde found that Mr. Godrick had been transferred there from Dedza. His name had been changed from 'Chinkhondo' to 'Che Lipanga' since he carried a spear wherever he went. We proceeded via the Liwawadzi River and Banda to Ncheu. Having climbed Ncheu, Dzunje and Dzobwe Mountains we went on to Fort Mlangeni only to learn that Chief Namulangeni had disregarded our advice, had moved his settlement westwards and had been apprehended by the Portuguese.

We travelled southwards, climbing Ntonda, Dzonzi, Tsangano, Manguo (the home of the Ambo people) and Tsambane mountains, following and marking the boundary all the way. Between the Linkhandwe and Mwanza rivers we could find no water and the fainting, thirsty carriers were sustained by the water which my wife carried in a big bottle on our journeys. Later, when we reached Salumbidwe, water became even more scarce and I was able to detect the existence of a pool of water only by carefully listening to the croaking of frogs. We could not camp nearby, however, because the pool was visited by many dangerous animals.

We followed the Mwanza River downstream and whilst on this part of our journey we sent all the womenfolk back to Zomba because the heat was too much for them. It was at this time that we also learned of the unfortunate death of Mr. Anderson, the Chief Surveyor, at Blantyre.

On reaching the Shire river we travelled downstream by canoe to Chiromo. The level of the water was too low to permit the passage of the river steamers. We stayed with Mr. Hilda, known as 'Mkwapatila', at Chiromo whilst the Portuguese Officers crossed the Ruo and stayed with their fellow countrymen for the night. The next day we went on to Port Herald which was under the charge of Captain Butcher. We worked near Port Herald, defining the boundary and then climbed Lulwe Hill. It was on this hill one evening that Mr. Swan shot and killed a most extraordinary looking wild goat. Its horns, legs and tail were those of a wild goat but the body and skin colouring were those of a leopard. One day when the carriers and machila-men were resting in the dry bed of the Tangadzi River masses of leaves and bushes were swept down upon them by the waters of the river which suddenly came up in spate. They lost their goods but saved their lives and I learned never to camp in a dry river bed.

We went on to the rivers Nkombedzi-wa-cuma and Nkombedzi-wa-fodya. The whole of this area at that time was suffering from famine and smallpox. Many Alomwe people coming to Nyasaland from Mozambique died of starvation. We spent three weeks with Mr. Virtue, the District Commissioner at Chikwawa, whilst the Europeans completed their boundary survey by drawing up and signing the final documents. I also signed as a witness. We travelled to Zomba, staying at the Mphembedzu, Mandala, and Namadzi resthouses.

Our journeys surveying the international boundary had taken us many months but we had all found it very interesting. In the same year that we completed it a meteorite fell at Naisi near Village Headman Chopi's village. The meteorite was inspected by Mr. Maclounie who tried to allay the fears of the people that it portended ill fortune during the coming year. The year was, however, one of peace and plenty.

Upon Mr. Anderson's death Mr. Binnie was appointed Chief Surveyor and I also was promoted to more responsible work, with a salary of £2 a month, a salary higher than that of any other African at the time. Three additional Europeans were also appointed to the Department: Mr. Wilson died on his arrival at Chinde but Mr. Kay and Mr. Bannerman arrived safely. This saw an increase in the amount of work undertaken by the Department. While Mr. Bannerman was supervising the construction of the water channel to the Residency in Zomba I accompanied Mr. Binnie and Mr. Kay to Karonga. Having walked to Liwonde, we boarded the steamer 'Duff' (known to Africans as 'Chikopa') and later, at the Fort Johnston bar, transferred to the Lake steamer 'Pania'. We called in at Monkey Bay, Domira Bay, Kota Kota, Likoma Island, Florence Bay and Deep Bay (Chitimba) before disembarking at Karonga where we surveyed various plots. We then travelled to Fort Hill (Chitipa) and surveyed plots for planters on the Luvira stream before returning to Karonga. Here we received the excellent news by telegram that the water channel to the Residency in Zomba had been completed and that the water was flowing satisfactorily. We sailed from Karonga and left Mr. Kay at Chinteche so that he could survey the Chinteche, Kasungu, Ngara and Dowa districts, whilst we returned to Zomba.

In 1902 I interrupted our surveying at Cholo and Port Herald to accompany Mr. Binnie to Chinde on the first part a his journey home to England on leave. I was taken aboard the ocean liner and was most surprised at everything I saw there. In November of that year I accompanied Sir Alfred Sharpe and Mr. Bannerman to Karonga so that we could survey the boundary between British and German territory. Together with some German surveyors we climbed Misuku Hill and then followed the Songwe River to Khambwe. This completed our survey and we returned to Zomba.

The year 1903 saw many changes; the Survey Department was renamed the Department of Public Works of which Mr. Binnie became the first Director and Mr. Fur was his Deputy. In that year Mr. Van set out the foundations of the Secretariat building.

In July 1903 we returned to Karonga to complete the survey of Nyasaland's borders by defining the Nyasaland-Northern Rhodesia boundary. We were helped in this work by surveyors from Northern Rhodesia. Later Mr. Binnie and Mr. Fur returned to Zomba but Mr. Bannerman and I carried on surveying in the Nyika plateau and then went on to visit Livingstonia Mission where we were hospitably received by Dr. Laws. Between 1903 and 1905 we surveyed in the Ngara, Kasungu, Mzimba

(District Commissioner Mr. Macdonald), Chinteche, Kota Kota and Dowa (District Commissioner, Mr. Green) Districts, and this saw the end of my land surveying work. In ten years I had walked all round Nyasaland's borders and covered much of its interior.

Most of my work after 1905 was concerned with road making. In April 1906, when I was the general capitao, I started to make the road from Domasi to Liwonde to join up with the Fort Johnston Road. The road capitao stationed at Domasi, Graham Kapeni, was later taken to work for Mr. Andrew and Mr. Bailey who were the first members of the Geological Survey in Nyasaland. In April 1907 we built the Mlunguzi bridge and then made the road from Zomba to Domasi.

In the following year, 1908, we surveyed first Zomba, then Blantyre and Chiromo townships. Later we began to survey the line of a road from Zomba to Fort Maguire. We had to climb Usenene (now called Ntonya), Zomba, Namikango, Mpyupyu, Sakata, Chaone and Malosa hills. Later we reached Madziabango and when we mounted Sonje Hill near Chief Chiwalo's village we were spat upon by red-necked flies which lived in the mbawa trees. The next day our faces and bodies were sore and swollen as if we had smallpox. Our disease became so bad that we could hardly see and walk. Dr. Harris from Fort Johnston, who eventually died of sleeping sickness, treated us and after three weeks we recovered. Later, when we were better, we travelled via Mangoche Hill, Chief Namwera's and on to Fort Maguire before returning to our home in Zomba.

During the dry season of 1909 we began to build the new road from Chinteche up to Mzimba. Much of the supervision and design of this road was left entirely to me because Mr. Bannerman had to go back to Zomba. Mr Moggeridge ('Mangulenji') was the District Commissioner at Chinteche at that time. Before the road work was completed I was called away to Fort Johnston but became ill and had to be carried to Zomba where I was admitted to the Livingstone Memorial Hospital of the Church of Scotland Mission and treated by Dr. Morris who had formerly been at the Blantyre Mission. After a few weeks I recovered and began work again. There were two main projects afoot, the construction of the road up to Zomba plateau and the remaking of the Zomba-Blantyre road. I was general capitao on both these jobs. We reached mile 11 on the Blantyre road in 1909, and Namaka at Mile 24 in 1910. In 1911 we reached Chichiri and joined up with the road which Mr. Shettle had made from Mile 31 via Lunzu, Ndirande and the Mudi stream to Chichiri. We also made an offshoot road from Mpingwe to Limbe Township.

The year 1912 began with the construction of the water channel tank at Zomba and then I was sent over to supervise the labourers making the road from Luchenza to Fort Lister. I also put two gangs at Fundi Cross to begin the road from there to Fort Anderson. We made this latter road to Lauderdale and Thornwood Estates right up to the Ruo river. When we got to the Palombe River on the Fort Lister road, however, I was summoned back to Luchenza to help make the Luchenza and Tuchila drifts. For a while I also helped Mr. Turnbull, the District Commissioner, Fort Anderson, to collect taxes.

Our work on the Mlanje roads continued during 1913 and 1914. In October 1914 it was rumoured that Chief M'mbelwa's people were refusing to pay taxes but soon we learned that the troubles were further north and were the beginnings of the First World War. Many Europeans and Africans went away to fight but I stayed in Nyasaland working on the roads.

ooo ☺ ☻ ooo

THE GOVERNOR-GENERAL AND THE LIVINGSTONIA ESCARPMENT

Lord Llewellyn, the first Governor-General of the Federation of Rhodesia and Nyasaland, visited Nyasaland soon after he took office. It was his wish that he visit as much of the country as possible and he was particularly keen to see the Northern Province.

The Provincial Commissioner and the District Commissioners planned the itinerary and, as a major part of it, included a visit to Livingstonia mission station. The mission was reached by a series of sharp hairpin bends rising in tiers that took the earth surface road up the steep escarpment from the Lake shore. The Governor-General travelled in a large black Humber Snipe car which was of such a length that it could not take the hairpin bends in one go but had to be reversed at each bend and then driven forward again. In some cases two or three such manoeuvres had to be made in order to get the car round the bend. As the car reversed, its tail end overhung the steep precipice and the driver had to apply his brakes very carefully. This was not a new problem nor a new solution, but it could be frightening for those who had not tackled it before. To minimize the danger of the brakes failing as the tail end of the car was extended out over the edge of the precipice, the District Commissioner arranged for one of his *boma* labourers to stand at the corner and, as the car reversed, to be ready to place a large boulder under one of the back wheels. It was a task he had performed a number of times before and as a result he had his own favourite boulder. The task, though sounding simple, in fact required a good deal of courage and strength and a steady nerve. Such qualities were in relatively short supply, and the District Commissioner needed a man in whom he could place complete trust. But the bends to be negotiated were numerous and there was only one man in whom the District Commissioner felt really confident. It was the man himself who proudly suggested the solution. Prefacing his proposal with the comments that he was well known to be a man of considerable strength and intelligence, who knew the escarpment as did no other and the road like the back of his hand, he offered – indeed demanded – that he stand at the first and lowest bend, ensure that the Governor-General's car safely negotiated it, and then, while the car was slowly being driven along the next stretch of road, he would clamber, with his boulder, straight up the slope and wait for the car to arrive, whereupon he would repeat the operation, wait for the car to move on and clamber up to the next bend, and so on until the top of the escarpment was reached. It was a prodigious effort, the task was successfully carried out and the labourer's name went down in local history.

Inside the Humber as it purred its tortuous way up to the mission station, the Provincial Commissioner pointed out to the Governor-General various items of interest in the landscape, and gave him an outline of the history of the place and especially of the mission. He also spoke of the way in which many members of the male population of the District had for decades emigrated to the mines and farms of South Africa and the Rhodesias to find paid employment. He was especially careful to divert the Governor-General's attention by conversation as each of the bends was negotiated, because he could see that Lord Llewellyn, who was known to have a weak heart, looked rather nervous and kept glancing out of the window as the car reversed at each bend.

In the fullness of time they reached the top of the escarpment and toured the mission, had tea and left to return, this time not via the escarpment road, to Provincial Headquarters where the Governor-General spent the night with the Provincial Commissioner and his wife. Over dinner Lord Llewellyn asked many questions about the Northern Province and seemed particularly interested in the social implications of so many of the menfolk leaving the area as emigrant labourers. With great sensitivity he hesitatingly enquired whether the loss of so many men led to a degree of inbreeding among the local communities. The question had never previously crossed the Provincial Commissioner's mind, despite the field studies carried out by a whole succession of social anthropologists in the past. Intrigued, he said that he did not think that the emigration led to inbreeding and asked why the Governor-General thought that it might. 'Ah, well,' said the noble lord, 'It is just that I thought all those men standing with boulders in their arms at each bend in the road this afternoon, looked remarkably like each other.'

THE POST OFFICE MESSENGER AND THE GOVERNOR

Justice is open to all, like the Ritz Hotel.
Lord Justice Mathew.

In March 1948 a new governor, Sir Geoffrey Colby, arrived in Nyasaland from Nigeria. He was young for a governor, enthusiastic, dynamic, highly development-oriented and 'raring to go'. His development strategy, which centred on rapidly increased production, also placed great importance on improved communications, including post and telegraph services.

The postal department, which at that time had 27 senior European members of staff and 359 junior African members of staff, must have seemed very small indeed to Colby after his Nigeria experience. It was a department which he was determined should increase in both size and in its contribution to the development drive. He was, however, aware of severe criticism of the department's activities being expressed both in the local press and in the legislature. The public, especially expatriate businessmen, were reaching exasperation point, the chamber of commerce pressed the Government to set up an official inquiry into the administration of the department, and the standing finance committee of Legislative Council recorded that 'the postal and telegraph services are the object of much justified public criticism.'

This was the scenario which Colby faced when he arrived, anxious and determined to develop the resources of the country as fully and as quickly as possible, and well aware of the vital importance of communications in the development process. He was immediately disturbed by much of what he heard about the postal department, not least its head, the Postmaster-General, and about the miscarriage of mail.

The Governor also had personal reasons for being disturbed by the state of the postal service: cheques sent for the payment of his daughters' school fees in Britain had gone astray in the post and a number of letters written by his wife to their daughters had not arrived. No doubt the headmistress and his daughters commented unfavourably on these apparent lapses, and neither as a newly appointed governor nor as a father would he have taken kindly to such comments. Complaints had also been received by the Standard Bank and from solicitors that their instructions were going astray. The Attorney-General claimed to have posted a number of personal cheques to Britain which had not arrived. Consequently Colby, whether for administrative-economic or personal reasons, raised the matter in Executive

Council on 1 July 1948. The advice which he received, and accepted, from council was that:

> The Commissioner of Police should be informed that postal matter is being stolen in the local post office to obtain the stamps thereon (especially one shilling and higher denomination stamps) for resale to stamp dealers, and he should be requested to make confidential enquiries through local stamp dealers with a view to ascertaining whether any of the stamps purchased by them have emanated from personnel of the postal department. The local philatelic societies should also be informed of the thefts and be asked to investigate the purchases of local stamps with a view to ascertaining who the local dealers are and from whom their purchases are made.

It is interesting that even at this early stage, the Executive Council seems to have known that letters were being stolen, as opposed to otherwise going astray, and where and why they were being stolen. The available evidence pointed to the mail being interfered with in the Zomba post office itself, since most of the complaints received were about mail posted in the capital and in most cases the letters were taken directly to the post office - in the case of Government House mail either by the Aide-de-Camp or by special messenger.

Additionally, the Attorney-General took two steps. First, at Colby's request, he carried out an inquiry by personally questioning post office headquarters staff and others who were in close contact with the Postmaster-General. The Postmaster-General - who rejoiced in the splendidly philatelic name of Wesley Rowland Hill Morgan - was aged 50 and had served with the Nyasaland Government since 1926 when he had transferred from the African Transcontinental Telegraph Company. He had been promoted Postmaster-General in 1946. He was reckoned by his senior colleagues to be 'an easy going sort of person but with a medical problem'; 'he had become "unwell" and took little interest in the running of the department'; 'his earlier abilities which he undoubtedly possessed had faded with middle-age and his indulgences, and he had lost the respect of his staff.' The Attorney-General conducted enquiries of senior postal staff about Morgan's administration, and these enquiries revealed many short-comings. The Chief Secretary - the head of the civil service - twice saw Morgan, cautioned him about his behaviour and suggested that he retire. Morgan initially resisted this suggestion so Colby had the question of his administration raised in Executive Council again and upon their advice he ordered that a commission of inquiry - which would have power to summon and examine witnesses in public - be set up to inquire into the administration of the postal department under the Commissions of Inquiry Ordinance with a judge of the high court as chairman, and members including a senior postal official from East Africa and a nominee of the Chamber of Commerce whose members had earlier pressed for an inquiry. The very next day Morgan left Zomba on retirement.

The Attorney-General's second step was to institute a prosecution for the theft of postage stamps. It was particularly the outgoing overseas mail, bearing higher denomination stamps, which was affected, and members of the Government must have noticed and been disturbed by a number of advertisements in the local press seeking large quantities of fine used current postage stamps for which dealers were offering - in the case of the higher denominations - five shillings per dozen.

Consequently, the Commissioner of Police sought the help of the Assistant Postmaster-General, John Lynn, whose office was located in the Zomba post office, and explained that the Governor had complained of his personal letters going astray. On 29 July the police showed Lynn five easily recognizable letters from the Governor, each bearing a one shilling stamp, and then at lunch time just before the mail was closed they posted the five letters in the Zomba post office letter box.

Lynn, whose office adjoined the sorting office, remained on the premises over the lunch hour when the van was due to arrive to take the mail to Blantyre, and kept watch through an aperture in the woodwork of the somewhat ancient door. From this peephole he could see the sorting frame into which the letters were sorted after collection from the post box and he knew exactly where the Governor's letters should be placed before being tied and put in the bag for Blantyre. As soon as the sorting was completed he left his office, went into the sorting office next door, checked the letters in the sorting racks and was unable to find the five Government House letters, which convinced him that they had been removed between the post box and the sorting racks. He immediately telephoned the police - who were awaiting his call - and they told him to instruct the clerk in charge that no one was to leave the sorting office until he gave permission. The police arrived shortly afterwards and searched all the employees and the inside of the post office but could not find the missing letters.

When the telephonists in a room adjoining the sorting office were questioned whether anyone had left the office via their room, they said that one of the messengers, Jereson, had done so and had returned whilst Lynn was on the phone. Jereson was questioned as to why he had left the office and he denied that there was any reason other than the need to visit the toilet.

Lynn, much perplexed, was convinced that the missing letters must have been taken outside the post office and hidden. There was a prolonged search and eventually he found the five letters - together with another addressed in Gujerati to India with a shilling and a sixpenny stamp on it - hidden underneath a drain which ran round the building. With this evidence, Jereson was again questioned and shown the letters and he then admitted to having stolen them and another from which he had torn two stamps before burning the letter.

The police went to Jereson's village and searched his hut and its surrounds. In the bush behind the hut they found two further letters bearing the Government House crest, from the envelopes of which the corner bearing the stamps had been torn off. These letters had been written some time previously by the Governor's wife to their daughters in Britain.

Jereson was arrested, admitted that he had been stealing stamps for many months and explained that he had originally done so at the instigation of a post office clerk who had subsequently been gaoled for theft of postal orders. He was in a favourable position to tamper with the mail because his duties included clearing - at no regular times - the post box, 'a wooden contraption propped up against the letter slit', which was not under lock and key or otherwise secured nor under any regular observation or supervision by senior officers. Access to it was via a large hole in its back and by simply pulling the box away from the wall. The sorting and sealing of mail was done by junior members of staff without close supervision by senior members, and the Attorney-General acknowledged that this system was justifiably open to adverse criticism.

Jereson was then aged 21 years and had been employed as a messenger for two years. His pay, until recently, had been twelve shillings a month, the equivalent re-sale value of thirty postage stamps. To double his income he needed only to steal one stamp a day. In the course of enquiries by the police it became clear that 'certain thoughtless persons' had in fact been paying high prices to Africans for used high denomination stamps for resale 'at a handsome profit to collectors in the United States of America and elsewhere.' The bona fides of these dealers was questionable since the particular denominations were seldom used internally but mainly for overseas mail and it was most improbable that the likes of Jereson could have come by such stamps, especially in large quantities, other than dishonestly.

Having apprehended Jereson, the Government decided to make an example of him, claiming that they had strong reason to believe that similar thefts were taking place in other post offices although senior officers of the postal department did not believe that theft of stamps from letters was a common practice. When Jereson joined the post office staff he should have been required by law to make a declaration before a magistrate and have his attention drawn to a schedule of offences including that with which he was now charged. This had not been done.

At his trial, less than a fortnight after Jereson's arrest, the Attorney-General himself appeared for the prosecution, before the resident magistrate. Jereson, who was unrepresented and who had no previous convictions, pleaded guilty to the charge of theft of postage stamps to the value of eight shillings. The Attorney-General pressed for 'a substantial and deterrent sentence' and the resident magistrate obliged: four years imprisonment with hard labour.

An examination of the July 1948 minutes of Executive Council, the *Nyasaland Times* reports of Jereson's trial, correspondence with Lynn and other senior postal officials and Arthur Loveridge's book, *I Drank the Zambezi* raises a number of puzzling and potentially disturbing questions about the case of Rex v. Jereson.

First is the question of the propriety of the personal intervention of the Governor and the Attorney-General. It is true that they were both members of the small Executive Council, the former having supreme responsibility for the good order and government of the country and the latter the responsibility for prosecuting offenders. Even so, the impression remains that the Governor may have been at least as irritated by the interference with his personal mail as by the damage threatened to the commercial activity of the Protectorate and to the reputation of the public service for efficiency and probity. For example, when the police first approached Lynn they said that the Governor 'had made a complaint that his personal letters were going astray somewhere'; and it was the opinion of at least one senior officer of the postal department that the Attorney-General's appearance for the prosecution was at the Governor's instigation. It is of course the case that the mere fact that the head of Government is the victim of criminal activity is no ground for not prosecuting, but one may think it imperative that he should play no personal part, either directly or indirectly, in the prosecution itself. The Attorney-General's behaviour is more open to criticism. In the first place, from time to time he acted as the Governor's Deputy. In the second place, he also was the victim of the same criminal activity and he need not himself have appeared for the prosecution since there were two crown counsel and a fairly large number of police officers who could have prosecuted. In the third place, astonishingly, he gave details to the court of his own personal letters which had gone astray and used the information in his address seeking a heavy sentence.

Next, there is the question of the unequal balance of representation before the court. On the prosecution side was the Attorney-General, the senior law officer, a solicitor-turned-barrister-at-law, 46 years of age with 24 years service behind him in three other colonial territories and in the Colonial Office, a highly trained and experienced lawyer who was to be made King's Counsel two years later. Since Jereson pleaded guilty the Attorney-General had virtually unlimited scope for giving his own version of the facts of the case when addressing the court. On the defence side was a 21 year old messenger of modest or no formal education, speaking little or no English - the language of the court - unrepresented and, because he pleaded guilty, unable to call witnesses to the facts of the case and in no position to challenge or comment on the lengthy account given by the Attorney-General. The Attorney-General's account differed in detail from the recollection of the Assistant Postmaster-General. Furthermore, the Attorney-General, who claimed that his own cheques went astray in the post, was himself heavily in debt and was being threatened by solicitors with legal proceedings.

Thirdly, it is remarkable that of all the stamps which Jereson admitted having stolen over a period of 'many months', only eight envelopes were found which had been misappropriated and seven of these were letters from the Governor or his wife, including the five he took on 29 July. Jereson admitted to having burnt only one letter; what happened to the others, if indeed others there were? Why should he have thrown only two letters - both from Government House and both written some time previously - in the bush behind his hut? Also, if Jereson admitted to stealing seven letters on the day he was apprehended, why did he remove stamps from only one of them and how did he have time to burn that letter?

Fourthly, to present day eyes, even if the Attorney-General was justified on grounds of public policy in seeking a 'substantial and deterrent sentence', in the circumstances four years hard labour for a first offence of stealing a few stamps seems excessive.

Finally, although the Government believed that the theft of stamps was widespread, only Jereson seems to have been proceeded against. The Executive Council was told that postal matter was being stolen 'in the local post offices'; a visitor to Nyasaland at the time was told by a senior member of the administration that 'some of the employees at Zomba post office' were awaiting trial for stealing stamps off letters; and the Attorney-General told the court that he had good reason to believe that thefts were taking place in other post offices. In particular, why were no stamp dealers prosecuted either for being accessories to the fact or being in possession of property reasonably suspected of having been stolen? In addressing the court, the Attorney-General made statements which seem to have indicated that he had material upon which to prosecute them.

Jereson who, once apprehended, was 'quite frank' with the prosecuting authorities, almost certainly revealed or could have revealed, the identity of the person to whom he sold the stolen stamps. Was he not asked, or did the Attorney-General decide not to prosecute the person named, and if the latter, why?

Is it possible that the real culprit, the person buying the stamps from Jereson, was a senior government official? An American academic visiting Nyasaland at the time was told by the District Commissioner of Blantyre that:

> some of the employees at Zomba Post Office were awaiting trial for lightly cancelling the picturesque shilling stamps so much used on air mail; then removing them from the envelopes and destroying the letters. Allegedly they were sold to someone in Zomba who was buying attractive Nyasa stamps from all the Native clerks in town. The stamps were then resold to dealers in the United States from whom the vendor was said to be receiving $140 a month.

The crucial words here are 'someone in Zomba'. It is unlikely that the Government would have been reluctant to prosecute non-officials all but a very few of whom were Asian traders. Being the capital and the seat of government, Zomba's overwhelming majority of inhabitants were senior, European, civil servants.

That it may have been a senior government official who was buying used stamps from African postal employees and then selling them on is entirely speculative and based on no cogent evidence, but it would fit the known facts and would help to explain why the matter was taken up in Executive Council, why Executive Council asked the Commissioner of Police discreetly to ascertain who the local dealers were when it was well known from advertisements in the local press who at least some of them were, why the Council told the Commissioner of Police how to conduct his investigation, why his enquiries were in confidence, why no prosecutions were made other than that of Jereson, why the prosecution was brought and concluded so quickly and why it was conducted by the Attorney-General himself, why the police did not try to pin the theft of stamps onto the clerk already convicted of theft of postal orders, and why Jereson was given such a long sentence - maybe to keep him out of circulation for a few years and to render any accusations he might make less credible. We shall never know - maybe fortunately.

Had Ian Hislop been aware of the case of Rex v. Jereson, he might well have made the comment he later uttered with disbelief on learning that the wife of the mass murderer Peter Sutcliffe had been awarded £600,000 libel damages against *Private Eye* of which he was the editor: 'If this is justice, I am a banana.'

BLACK PEARLS

Knowledge comes, but wisdom lingers.
Tennyson.

I

You Europeans are a funny set of people. For example, you correctly extol the beauties of our mountains and you like to live close to them. Yet instead of building your houses so that they face the mountains which you admire so much and which you could enjoy if you were able to look at them, what do you do? You turn their backs on the mountains and face your houses outwards across the plains which, again you correctly say, are far less interesting, leaving the enjoyment of seeing the mountains to your domestic staff living at the back of your houses.

And another example. Why is it that you so build your houses that when guests arrive they nearly always arrive at the back of the house near the kitchen where they park their cars and then have to walk round to the front of the house to be greeted? Would it not be better to have them drive round to the front of the house so that you can welcome them properly?

Also, you spend a good deal of money on beautiful material for your curtains: colourful material with lovely patterns on it, material in which you can be justly proud. Yet, again, what do you do? You hang the curtains so that the patterned side is facing inwards, thereby presenting the plain, dull, uninteresting, side to the public. You might just as well buy really cheap material.

Yet again, on the Lake shore and in the Lower River, in the hot season you arrange 'hot station hours'. You start work at 7.00 a.m., which is sensible, and you take the afternoon off, but only from 1.00 p.m. onwards, which is not sensible since you are then working through the hottest part of the day, that is at and just after noon.

Consider, too, your oft repeated advice about hygiene and sanitation. The typical colonial dwelling has the lavatory inside the house and the kitchen in a small building outside. We, on the other hand, cook inside our house and have our lavatory in a small building outside.

II

On learning that his employer had been awarded the MBE, the District Commissioner's head servant remarked kindly, 'That's very good, but let us not forget that one medal does not chink!'

III

The *boma* carpenter's advice to a young apprentice was that if he held the hammer with both hands he would avoid hitting his thumb with it.

IV

It is foolish to pay your tax before the date on which you have to, for you may die before that date and would lose your money. Similarly, why plant a mango tree in your old age? You will never benefit from it.

V

Dr. Banda's advice to young graduates on the need for practical experience was that to learn to swim it was no good people doing so on Mulanje Mountain: they should go down to the Lake and get into the water.

VI

Dr. Banda's calculated advice to the Africans of South Africa during the apartheid regime was to be glad of what they could get, realize that half a loaf is better than no loaf and not expect to get all they wanted at once. 'You should accept half a loaf this year, demand half next year and the other half in the following year.'

VII

A fancy new government town will not materially improve the diets of the hungry people in the villages. Expensive government palaces and limousines have never notably reduced the infant mortality rate. Henry Chipembere, *The Guardian* 7 July 1966.

VIII

To pull oneself up by one's boot straps, one first needs boot straps.

IX

A young man was listening intently to a High Court Judge at a drinks party recounting his exploits during World War II. The Judge was particularly proud of the way in which he had escaped three times from a

German prisoner of war camp, and he dwelt at length on his prowess in doing so. He then turned to the young man, smiled, raised one eyebrow and awaited his reaction. The young man hesitated, looked thoughtful and then asked slowly, 'But doesn't that mean, Sir, that you were *captured* three times?'

X

When I went to Makanga experimental station I was shown beautiful onions by a young agricultural officer there. All very well but I asked 'Are you selling these onions anywhere?' He said 'No!' I asked him 'Why not? What is the point of producing these onions if you are not going to sell them?' Dr. Banda in Parliament October 1967.

ooo ☺ ☻ ooo

WHITE FATHERS

I

During tea at one of the senior seminaries in the Protectorate a visitor enquired how long some of the European priests, the White Fathers, had been in the country. He was fascinated to be told that the longest serving father had been there for thirty one years, and he was astonished to learn that during the whole of that time the old man had not once returned to his homeland in France. He asked how long the others had been there, and the number of years varied from one or two to twenty, but they all, save for the very youngest, had returned to their homes at fairly regular, though not frequent, intervals. The visitor was told that not more than one priest at a time was allowed to go on furlough and this meant that the turn of each of them came round infrequently. Asked why only one priest at a time was permitted to go on leave to their home in Europe, the old priest - he who had never returned to his home - explained, 'Well, you see, when we do go back to Europe, even if it is for a short time, we are required to visit the Vatican. For such a visit, of course, we have to be attired subfusc and, since we have only one dark suit between us, we have to wait for one of us to return to the seminary before another of us can leave.'

II

At another White Fathers' seminary, a young priest was about to take a driving test and he told his Superior that he was rather worried with the prospect. He assured the Superior - a saintly man of great compassion, wisdom and understanding - that his concerns were not because he doubted the road worthiness of the seminary's ancient and much repaired car in which he was to sit the test, but because, being French and his English not being of the best, he frequently confused right with left. 'My son', the Superior gently said, 'Have no fear. When we cross ourselves, the invariable sequence is head, abdomen, left chest, right chest. It is a sequence we never forget. So, if you are asked to turn left, simply remember this sequence and all will be well.' The young priest thanked the Superior for his sound and practical advice and left much reassured. A few days later the priest sat the driving test and on his return to the seminary the Superior was disappointed to see him looking uncomfortable and downcast. He asked what had happened, and received the reply: 'Father, I was doing very well until the last moment when I was asked to take the next turning left. Following your advice, I remembered the sequence of movements with which we cross ourselves. Indeed, to make absolutely sure, I actually crossed myself, and I was failed for lack of confidence!'

ooo ☺ ☻ ooo

ARRIVALS AND DEPARTURES

I

SIR HARRY JOHNSTON'S ARRIVAL

Harry Johnston's first arrival in Blantyre was somewhat undignified if dramatic, and he described it in amusing terms in his autobiography:

'Arrived at Katunga, I found Mr. John Moir awaiting me. He had brought down with him for my conveyance a wild mare - The Nightmare, I subsequently named her, after several years' experience – who, supposing me to be an equestrian, might convey me speedily over the twenty-eight miles of rough mountain road leading up from Katunga to Blantyre, an ascent of nearly three thousand feet. This mare apparently realized that there was a possibility of meeting tsetse fly on the river level of Katunga, so no time must be wasted there. I was no sooner on her back than she made for the ascending road and seemed to me to gallop the whole way up it till she reached the outside of her stable at 'Mandala', the African Lakes Company's suburb of Blantyre. The rotten leather bridle came to pieces, and before I could clutch at the two ends they had fallen to the ground, the horse had put its foot on them, snapping them off, and there I was on its back, without any means of controlling the animal.

I managed fortunately to remain on her back, but the approach to Mandala made me feel deep sympathy for Mazeppa. There were avenues that overarched, pergolas that were too low, and my attitude as the mare flew with me up to her stable door - and not to the front of the mansion where a deputation was waiting to receive me - was crouched and clinging. I surprised Mrs. Moir very much by walking into her kitchen from the back premises and explaining who I was.'

Thus, bleeding, bruised and battered, arrived Her Britannic Majesty's Commissioner and Consul-General, and the founder of the British Central Africa Administration. Johnston later said he regarded his ride from Katunga to Blantyre as quite the greatest risk he ever ran in British Central Africa.

II

SIR GEOFFREY COLBY'S ARRIVAL AND DEPARTURE

On 7 January 1948 the newly appointed governor of Nyasaland, Sir Geoffrey Colby, sailed from England for Africa, through the Mediterranean and the Suez Canal down the east coast to Beira and thence by train to Limbe. What might have been his expectations for his arrival? The general standard in the British colonies was that on leave and on other ceremonial occasions, there was a guard of honour to greet the Governor on his arrival and departure. Senior officials were required to turn up at the railway station or airport to bid farewell and welcome. Indeed, colonial governors were entitled to a 17-gun salute on arrival and departure.

The standard which Colby knew best, that set in Nigeria, where he had previously served, was impressive. An observer of Sir Bernard Bourdillon's arrival as the new governor recorded:

> On the morning of his arrival we all went down to the Customs wharf, the men in white uniform and the ladies superb in their best; ... the Commissioner of Police held his drawn sword. The wharf was alive with bunting in a brisk wind. The Regiment mounted one of its immaculate guards of honour and the band played on a flank. The guns fired their slow salute from across the water. The Aide de Camp appeared first, setting the standard of the show with his full-dress Lancer uniform. Then the tall figure of Sir Bernard came

> down the companion way in his blue uniform and plumes, with his dazzling wife. They shook hands with all those entitled and drove off to Government House.

Similarly, the standard set in Nigeria in gubernatorial rail travel was impressive:

> Travelling by rail was the most luxurious, for the Governor had his own train, consisting of six coaches, the Governor's with a lounge and two bedrooms, one for his Aide de Camp and Private Secretary, one for the servants, another comprising the dining-saloon and kitchen and a baggage coach for the Governor's car, luggage and supplies. Just before breakfast the train stopped in the middle of nowhere because His Excellency must not be joggled whilst he is eating.

In Northern Nigeria the Governor's comfortable special train of two white coaches contained a drawing room and dining room seating a dozen people; the two bedrooms had 'real beds' and a bathroom with a long bath; and there was a flat coach for five cars.

In Tanganyika, where Colby called on the Governor on his way to Nyasaland, the Governor's rail coaches contained, in the first, 'two bedrooms with real beds and Dunlopillo mattresses, a bathroom with a long bath, a small drawing room and an observation car', and, in the other, 'a dining room for eight, two bedrooms and bathroom for private secretary and housekeeper, kitchen and pantry' in addition to a van for the band and two trucks for the motor cars.

These, the Nigerian and the Tanganyikan, standards were the only ones personally known to Colby and it may be that he was expecting a similar, albeit possibly scaled down, version in Nyasaland. His journey from Beira to Limbe was by rail in the Nyasaland Railways' General Manager's coach. In ideal conditions this journey, a distance of some 350 miles, could be both beautiful and fascinating. Since the Governor's aide-de-camp, Robert Tait Bowie, and Misapo, a very old man who had been personal servant to a series of governors, had travelled to Beira to accompany and assist the new governor and his wife on the last stage of their journey to Nyasaland, it ought to have been so for the Colbys. But in colonial Nyasaland, as elsewhere, things occasionally fell short of what they ought to be.

The passenger train left Beira twice weekly and 'for the first hour or so crawled through swamps of blue lotus lilies and past banana and copra plantations' to Dondo, a quiet Portuguese station, the junction of the lines from Rhodesia and Nyasaland. After an hour's wait at Dondo, the train travelled for several hours through the lower Zambezi valley. In the late 1940s the train left Beira at 5.00 p.m. and this part of the journey was usually made at night.

Shortly before their arrival the next morning at Chiromo, towards the end of the rainy season, a vast island of floating vegetation, which officials and engineers tried in vain to break up with timber saws and explosives, had swept down the swollen Shire river relentlessly carrying all, including the Chiromo railway bridge, before it. This calamity necessitated the passengers leaving their train on the west bank, crossing the fast flowing river by temporary ferry, and joining another train on the east bank - an irritating, uncomfortable, and in many ways alarming exercise for the new arrivals.

Just after the train left the last station before Limbe, the final stop, the Colbys began to prepare themselves for their arrival and the new governor called for Misapo to lay out his clothes, but Misapo did not answer: he had got off the train at the last station to buy himself some bananas with which to fortify his inner self for the important arrival at Limbe, and had been left behind. Since during his prep school, public school and university days, though less frequently during his Nigeria days, Colby had managed without a personal servant, he was easily able to cope with this minor, if unexpected, set-back, but the demons of natural cussedness had not yet retired for the day – even one as important as this.

For reasons then, and now, unknown to others, but possibly connected with the earlier delays at Chiromo, Tait Bowie - who 'kept popping in and out with changed plans' - believed that the train was running late on its final stages up the Shire Highlands escarpment. A considerate man, well accustomed to the way of life in Nyasaland and not wishing unnecessarily to inconvenience his senior colleagues, Tait Bowie telegraphed a message to Limbe saying that the train would be late. Recollections vary as to the reported length of delay. The Chief Justice's wife recalled:

> The Colbys arrived in Limbe on a Sunday afternoon. We were all teed up to meet them when we were informed that the train was three hours late (nothing unusual on that wood-fired line especially if there was a 'chip' blowing). So we settled down to a Sunday afternoon zizz. No sooner were we on our beds when the phone rang and we were told that the train had made up time and was due in Limbe in twenty minutes. Maybe someone had blundered and the train had not lost time. So there was a terrific scramble to get to Limbe before the train - we just made it.

Apart from the Chief Justice and his wife, the police officer who had phoned them, and the Provincial Commissioner, who rushed panting onto the platform in the nick of time as the train pulled in, none of the other invited guests was present to greet the Colbys on their first arrival in Nyasaland. As Lady Colby, reminiscing many years later, recalled:

> It was all rather a contrast after travelling somewhat royally in a special coach with every comfort between Mombasa and Nairobi! In all one was taken down a peg or two.

Eight years later, Colby celebrated his fifty-fifth birthday and two days later, on 25 March 1956, he left Nyasaland for England and retirement. With Lady Colby and their younger daughter, Carol, he left Government House in Zomba at about eight o'clock in the morning and travelled to Limbe, where they reached the railway station at nine o'clock. There was a large crowd of Europeans - the women in smart dresses, the men in suits - and a number of equally well dressed Asians and Africans to bid them farewell. As Colby stepped from the large black Buick, the police band struck up the royal salute, the national anthem, and the well-drilled guard of honour presented arms. For the last time he was accorded the formal respect due to the Queen's personal representative in the Protectorate. He briefly inspected the police contingent and then, almost as briefly, said goodbye to as many of those present as he reasonably could. Lady Colby did the same and had time for a kindly word with even the most junior Assistant District Commissioner present. Colby, tall and erect, took it all smartly and naturally. Lady Colby, when she spoke, seemed tired and rather upset at leaving. Carol looked relieved that the whole affair was nearly over.

They climbed aboard the waiting train and, as on their arrival, occupied the General Manager's private coach, waving goodbye from the observation platform at the rear of the train as it puffed gently and pulled slowly away from the station. On the platform people lingered for a while and quietly chatted; the Acting Chief Justice anguished publicly over whether it was proper for him to administer the oath to the Acting Governor before the Governor himself had actually crossed the Protectorate's frontier with Mozambique.

Colby was not best pleased when he reached Britain to receive a bill from the General Manager of the Nyasaland Railways charging him for the use of the coach, as if to remind him that the railways were still in private, commercial, hands – the Governor had clandestinely tried to nationalize the railways a few years earlier. They were able to smile at this pettiness, but decades later Lady Colby remembered it and coupled it with the occasion upon which she officially launched the Nyasaland Railways' steamer 'Ilala' and was graciously rewarded for her trouble by the General Manager presenting her with a box of chocolates of modest dimensions!

ooo ☺ ☻ ooo

MBALAME THE BIRD MAN

Shall I call thee bird or but a wandering voice?
Wordsworth.

An almost daily task of a District Commissioner and his Assistants was the hearing of 'complaints' – *madandaula.* At these sessions, representations would be made, or advice would be sought, by a great variety of Malawians on a great many different subjects. One could rarely tell in advance what sort of subjects would be raised. The complainants would line up on the *khonde* of the District Office; they might or might not be 'sorted' by the head clerk but they were always shown in, one individual at a time, by a messenger, usually the head messenger. Sometimes the complainant would be accompanied by his village headman. The complainant or, if he were accompanied, the village headman, would state what it was that was concerning them – often at considerable length and with many digressions so that the story should be fully understood – and the DC or ADC would try to work out how the matter should best be handled. Sometimes they were able to deal with the matter immediately and satisfactorily, sometimes their advice was to take the question to the local court or the chief for adjudication, and at others - more rarely - to return to the village and sort matters out themselves. At times the DC or ADC would tell the complainant that there seemed to be no substance in the matter that they had raised and that they should go home and try not to bother him again. Very occasionally a complainant would bring to the *boma* a particularly interesting and worrying case. One such was the case of the Bird Man.

Accompanied by his village headman, a villager told the DC that his three year old daughter had been missing from home for almost a month. He, his relatives and fellow villagers had searched far and wide and had made many enquiries but no one was able to help them to find the girl. He was clearly distraught and at the end of his tether. The DC asked several questions and was at a loss to decide what advice he could give. He said that the searches should continue and he promised to speak with the officer in charge of police to see if he could help. Only partly comforted, the man and his headman left the DC's office.

They had just departed when the head messenger asked to see the DC and said that he believed the child could be found by the Bird Man. He went on to explain to the astonished DC – for the head messenger was a man who had previously always had his feet firmly on the ground – that in a village not too far away, *patali pang'ono,* there lived a man who turned himself into a bird and in the course of flying long distances discovered many things unknown to others. Undoubtedly he could find the missing child, if asked by the DC. If anyone else had told him this profoundly improbable story, the DC would have suggested that he visit a local medicine man and get his head examined. But the DC had known the head messenger for many years, since indeed they had served together in the KAR during the war, and – still incredulous – he patiently asked the head messenger to tell him more. The head messenger said there was little more to tell except that he would be happy to ask the Bird Man to come and see the DC. When the DC asked him to do this, the head messenger said it was not as straight forward as it might be supposed. 'How's that?' enquired the DC and received the reply 'Well, he's in the prison, and getting him here will require your authority, since you are also the officer in charge of the prison.' The DC was reluctant to get involved officially in what was almost certain to turn out to be a hare-brained scheme. The head messenger, seeing the DC's discomfort, said that, if it were agreeable, he would act unofficially and ask the head warder at the prison to release the Bird Man in order that he could call on the DC. He added that this would not be a problem and that the head warder would not even need to escort the Bird Man, because he knew that the fellow could fly out of the prison any time he liked, on several occasions had done so and had always returned voluntarily and as promptly as circumstances permitted. The DC, now even more doubtful of ever having allowed this conversation to begin, told the head messenger to go ahead and see what he could do.

A few days later, the head messenger slipped quietly into the DC's office and said, 'He's here'. 'Who?' enquired the DC whose mind was on writing the district annual report, now almost a month late. 'The Bird Man, *Bwana*. By the way, his real name is Mbalame.' 'OK. Bring him in – or would he prefer to fly?' 'How droll' thought the head messenger in Chinyanja, though he did not say so, and shortly he returned with a smallish, thin, man with an unusually black, narrow featured and gently smiling face and closely shaven head. The DC invited him to sit down but – presumably, the DC thought, because birds rarely actually sit down – he said he preferred to stand, presumably, the DC further thought, on one leg. When asked if he could find the missing child, Mbalame confidently, yet strangely humbly, said that he could. Further gently pressed as to how he would do this since everyone else, including now the police, had failed, he explained that he would turn himself into a bird and would fly in ever increasing circles looking carefully down for any signs of the child until he found her. He would then tell the head messenger where she was and the head messenger would go and collect her and return her to her family. The DC said that he would be very pleased if Mbalame would help in this way, and his visitor then left him.

About a fortnight later, the DC's writing of his now even more belated annual report was interrupted by the entry of the head messenger who, broadly smiling, told him that the Bird Man had discovered the missing child; that he, the head messenger, had climbed a remote hill to a cave where he found the child, warm, well and safe. She had been abducted, but in no way harmed, by a childless couple from a village in the neighbouring district who had run away when the messenger approached the cave and they could not now be found. He had returned the little girl to her parents who were, naturally, much relieved and delighted. The DC was equally delighted and asked if Mbalame could come and see him so that he could thank him.

After a few days delay – because the Bird Man thought he had been away from prison too long recently and this was resented by, and was the subject of complaint from, his fellow inmates – he came to the *boma* and was shown into the DC's office by the head messenger. The DC thanked him and, still deeply puzzled, asked him how he had done it. 'I did it, as I said I would, by turning myself into a bird, flying in greater and greater circles until I found the child. She was in a cave on a hill and that is where I found her and told your head messenger.' 'But how do you turn yourself into a bird?' enquired the DC. Mbalame shifted from foot to foot, scratched his bald head, looked furtively over his shoulder and said, 'I just do it. Would you like to see?' When the DC said he would, the Bird Man told him there was a problem because he could only do it at night, in darkness. Not to be thwarted, the DC said he could close the curtains of his office and this would make it quite dark. He said this with little confidence, because the heavy green curtains had never before been drawn closed, and in any case he did not for one moment believe that Mbalame would call his bluff. None the less, the Bird Man agreed, the curtains were drawn closed and, at Mbalame's insistence, the window was left open. The DC waited anxiously, closing his eyes to become accustomed to the darkness. When, after a moment or two, he opened his eyes, the Bird Man took an unbelievably long and deep breath, began to suck in his now remarkably hollow cheeks, stuck his lips forward an extraordinary distance and indeed did begin to look distinctly bird-like facially. The impression was deepened when Mbalame drew his black and somewhat ragged jacket up over his narrow shoulders and, gripping the cuffs, began to flap his arms - or wings - in a most convincing bird-like fashion. He moved - hopped - towards the window, ready to fly out as the DC was now firmly beginning to believe. The flapping of the wings increased. One foot was already off the ground. All was silent save for the sound of the flapping wings and the DC's heavy and rapid breathing. Suddenly the spell was broken, there was a knock at the door and the ADC entered, excusing himself for interrupting the DC's interview. It took a few seconds for the DC to recover his composure and, as it were, come down to earth. When he did so he was astonished to find that only the head messenger was still in the office with him. The Bird Man had disappeared.

ooo ☺ ☻ ooo

CULINARY CATASTROPHES

Kissing don't last; cookery do.
George Meredith.

I

The young Agricultural Officer at Chikwawa was to be visited by the Director of Agriculture who would arrive mid-morning, stay for lunch, inspect the cotton fields in the afternoon and then depart to return to headquarters. The Agricultural Officer, a bachelor, was keen to give his head of department a good lunch, partly to make up for any deficiencies that the Director might discover in matters agricultural. He decided on a rather splendid menu for the meal: vegetable soup, roast duck with potatoes, cabbage and carrots, followed by a mango fool desert, the whole to be accompanied by a bottle – or two – of Portuguese rosé wine. He checked with his cook that all the ingredients were available and that the cook had no qualms about producing the meal successfully.

The evening before the Director's visit the Agricultural Officer instructed his kitchen boy to go to a nearby village and purchase a duck. He gave him £1 for this purpose and repeated his instructions in Chinyanja. The kitchen boy went out very early in the morning to buy the duck but was back well before the Director arrived and in good time for the bird to be cooked. He returned with his purchase in a sack in which it was moving vigorously. The Agricultural Officer, accompanied by his cook, asked to see the duck. Both were smiling in anticipation, the one at the prospect of impressing his Director contemporaneously with enjoying a better than usual meal, the other in anticipation of impressing both his employer and the 'Big *Bwana* from Zomba' and shortly thereafter enjoying the left-overs from the meal. One might suppose that the kitchen boy would also be in a good mood for he almost certainly had paid less than the pound he had been given for the purchase, and he too might well have been anticipating joining the cook in the left-overs. In fact, he felt none of these emotions and indeed was baffled by the whole affair. None the less, he gently lifted the sack, undid the string holding it closed, and turned it upside down. There was a blurred dark flash and a terrified screech as a black cat leapt out of the sack and raced off into the bush.

When he had regained some of his composure, and had speedily changed the lunch menu from roast duck to corned beef pie, the Agricultural Officer demanded of the kitchen boy an explanation for bringing a cat instead of a duck. The explanation was, eventually, a simple one: the kitchen boy, gravely puzzled but assuming that the Agricultural Officer knew what he was talking about, had understood his employer to have asked him to purchase an *mphaka*, a cat, and not a *bakha*, a duck.

II

The Dona was suffering from a very heavy cold and none of the remedies that she took seemed to do any good. Finally, in her misery she reflected back to her childhood days when she did not, so far as she could recall suffer from colds or any other childhood ailments, though, now that she came to think of it, her mother often did have colds. Maybe it was hereditary. It was while thinking about those far off days that she suddenly recalled that her mother had used an inhalant called, what was it? – Ah, Yes, Friars Balsam. She could see her mother now, pouring into a basin of boiling water a few drops of the balsam, which turned to a deep dark brown colour and gave off steaming vapours. Her mother would place the bowl on the kitchen table, lean her face closely over it, cover her head with a towel and spend several minutes deeply breathing in the vapours. She avowed that it did her a power of good, and certainly she seemed more cheerful after using the balsam. Did anyone sell Friars Balsam in Nyasaland? A few telephone calls to the nearest town resulted in her finding a pharmacy that did indeed sell the balsam, and they agreed to send a bottle of it to her straightaway. It arrived the following day. She was delighted and even more pleased when, having inhaled the vapours for several minutes she felt very much better, so much better indeed that she was able to enjoy a long siesta – a treat which the cold had denied her for the past several weeks.

When she awoke from her slumbers she rang for the cook and asked him to bring tea to her bedroom and – as a further treat, she would like a slice of the fruit cake she had baked the previous day. The cook had experienced the sharp end of his mistress's tongue this past week when her cold was at its heaviest and her temper at its shortest, and he hastened to comply as quickly as he could with her request. He was a thrifty man and frequently retained the contents of the tea pot used earlier in the day, by pouring them into a basin which he kept in the corner of the kitchen and then heating them up for his own tea break. Occasionally, when his employers were in a hurry, he would take a short cut and heat up the stale tea in a saucepan, pour it into the tea pot, place it on the tray and take it to them. They did not seem able to tell the difference.

And he took the short cut on this occasion, placing the re-heated tea in its pot, together with a generous slice of fruit cake on a tray, covered the whole with a bead fringed muslin cloth and took it to his mistress. She beamed in anticipatory pleasure, and when the cook left, settled down to enjoy the tea and cake. Outside, the cook heard first a disconcerted mumbling and then a high pitched screech: 'Cookie, come here at once! This damned tea tastes foul. It's like drinking Friars Balsam! Come here at once!' But the cook, blessed with a pragmatic wisdom borne of long service in European households, had already fled!

III

The Governor was paying a visit to one of the Districts in the very north of the country and the District Commissioner planned a full official programme together with an almost as full social programme for His Excellency, who was to be accompanied by his wife. The highlight and climax of the social programme was to be dinner on the last night of the visit at the District Commissioner's house, to which a dozen or so senior officials and half a dozen non-civil service members of the local community were to be invited.

The DC's young wife energetically set about making arrangements for the dinner, and thought – having read history at university - she would like to give the meal a 'mediaeval' flavour. She laughingly dismissed the fleeting temptation that her small daughter's nanny might dress as a serving wench, and concentrated on the food itself. There was even to be mead which she was sure she could make from beer and local honey; she tried it and it worked splendidly, much to her husband's pleasure and her relief. The *piece de resistance*, however, was to be a young suckling pig, roasted whole and brought to the table on a plank covered with foil. The young pig was purchased and, the day before the dinner, it was killed and slowly roasted over a charcoal fire outside the kitchen, under the close supervision of the mistress of the house. So well did the arrangements go that she was bubbling with excitement and confidence and was much looking forward to the evening.

As the guests arrived for dinner and the Governor and his wife entered the lounge, she had one last check in the kitchen to see that everything was still going well. It was, and she carefully repeated to the cook what she had already told him several times: in the olden days in the great baronial halls of England suckling pigs were served, and were usually brought to the dining hall with great ceremony, the roasted pig being carried on a large silver platter and its head decorated with an orange in its mouth and a stick of celery behind each ear. Was the cook sure he understood this? He was quite sure: the pig was to be brought to the table with a stick of celery behind each ear and an orange stuck in the mouth. Good!

Drinks before dinner went well, the guests mingled nicely and the Governor and his wife were very much at their ease. The DC's wife moved easily from one guest to another and her husband thought how lucky he was to have her. They all sat down to dinner, the Governor on his hostess's right, his wife on the DC's right. The mead was popular, and after the soup was consumed the great moment arrived. The guests had learned that there was to be something very special for the main course, and there was a babble of excitement followed by a hushed silence as the door was opened and the splendid roast suckling pig was carried in shoulder high by the cook, clad in his immaculately white *khansu* and bright red fez, with a stick of celery behind each of his ears and an orange stuffed in his mouth.

IV

Given the importance of food in our lives, it is not surprising that it should have played an important part in ballads, legends and folk tales from the earliest times. What is rather surprising, however, is that it has also been found in a few recently discovered palaeolimericks:

A nutritionist speaking in Dedza
when asked 'Please repeat what you just said, Sir.'
replied 'You must eat lots of beans,
cabbage, fresh meat and greens,
with oranges, mangos and *mtedza.*

A gourmet from village Mtalika
planted capsicums up on the Nyika.
He enjoyed food a lot
especially when hot
and seasoned his beer with paprika.

An amorous young man from Mbame
set out one evening to charm me.
We went out to dine
and after some wine
he suggested a plate of salami.

An uncouth young fellow from Chapananga
ate his meals with a rusty old panga.
His mother said, 'Sonny,
you've plenty of money
so buy a new knife *msanga sanga.*

An extravagant gourmet from Kuntaja
ate *nyama* from a fine silver charger.
His friends thought he showed off,
by behaving like a toff
just like a grand maharaja.

ooo ☺ ☻ ooo

QUEEN ELIZABETH, THE QUEEN MOTHER

The visit to Nyasaland of Elizabeth the Queen Mother in 1960 caused a great deal of excitement, and many accounts of it were written and publicized: accounts of the way in which she mesmerized the crowd at the Zomba Gymkhana Club by wearing pale blue evening dress with tiara and decorations that glittered in the bright morning sunshine; and tales of how captivated she was by the views from the top of Zomba Plateau, especially those from a particular vantage point, named thereafter, as it still is today, 'Queen Elizabeth View'. There are, however, two stories about this royal visit that are less well known.

I

During the visit the Governor, Sir Robert Armitage, and his wife, Lyona, celebrated their thirtieth wedding anniversary. They did so quietly so as not to detract from the Queen Mother's visit – and indeed there would have been little opportunity to do otherwise. The anniversary was mentioned to the Queen Mother and she congratulated them and hoped they would enjoy many more happy years of married life together. Thirty years later, when the Armitages were in retirement in Wiltshire, they celebrated their sixtieth wedding anniversary – a simple affair with their sons arranging a quiet luncheon with their closest family and a few friends. As Sir Robert and Lyona were getting ready for the luncheon they were surprised to see arrive at the front door a large black car, from which a grey suited chauffeur emerged carrying a huge basket of the most beautifully arranged and colourful flowers. The chauffeur asked to see Sir Robert and his wife and explained to them that he had come from Clarence House in London with the flowers from the Queen Mother – whom they had not seen for three decades – together with her best wishes for their diamond wedding anniversary.

II

The Sunday afternoon of the Queen Mother's visit was left free of official engagements, and Lady Armitage arranged to take their royal visitor to the home of an old settler family who lived about ten miles from Zomba on an estate which they had farmed for many years. It was to be a quiet afternoon at which tea would be taken *en famille.* All went well, and the Queen Mother chatted easily with the widow – now an elderly lady - of the first owner of the estate, her son and daughter-in-law and their children – who, to their mother's relief, behaved unusually well. After tea, the old lady asked the Queen Mother, 'Would you mind, Ma'm, if I did a little sewing?' The Queen Mother, herself an accomplished needlewoman, said that she too enjoyed needlework and asked if she could help. The old lady smiled sweetly, shook her head gently and then reached behind her chair, drew out a well-worn leather saddle, placed it on her lap and proceeded to repair it with a nine inch curved needle.

III

As a postscript, there is also the story of the Queen Mother's earlier visit to Nyasaland in 1957. At a garden party during that visit she was introduced to two European 'old timers' who had lived in the country for many, many years and both of whom had very large families still living there. One of them, a great-grandmother, had thirteen children - six boys and seven girls - of whom she was very proud. The other, also a great-grandparent, had twelve children - six boys and six girls - of whom he was equally proud. Indeed there had been an element of rivalry between the two until, with the passage of time and the death of their respective spouses, they began to accept the status quo. This process was helped by the remarkable coincidence that they had an equal number of grandchildren and great grandchildren, but with the potential for further great-grandchildren to be born the issue was still a live one.

When these two ancient worthies were presented by the Governor to the Queen Mother, she said that she understood they both had very large families and how very proud of them they must be. She followed these remarks by asking how many children they actually had. The old lady, longing for Her Majesty to ask this just question, had her reply ready and said sweetly, 'I have thirteen children, Ma'am, and my friend here has only twelve.' Anticipating such an upstaging remark, the old man also had his answer ready: 'Yes, Your Majesty, that is so, and the reason is that, unlike the late lamented husband of our dear friend here, I was away during the First World War, fighting for my King and country, and unable during that period to fulfil my marital duties.'

ooo ☺ ☻ ooo

WELL – PERHAPS JUST A LITTLE ODD

The Colonial Service in Nyasaland produced its fair share of eccentrics both in the earliest days of the protectorate, and throughout the colonial era. Among these were the following.

I

There were a number of unconventional characters in Sir Harry Johnston's Administration in the 1890s. The attire of some was remarkable; there was, for example, 'a man getting on in years, of decent birth and breeding, a University graduate, dressed in nothing but spectacles and a bath towel.' Then there were the two officials who startled Reginald Maugham at dinner on his first night in Zomba; one was attired in a long frock coat, a canary-coloured waistcoat with silver buttons, a white tie, black trousers and patent leather shoes; the other wore an evening dress coat and waistcoat, long tie of dark green tastefully relieved by small yellow flowers, grey trousers, and brown boots. Even Gilbert Stevenson, normally not a flamboyant person, irritated Edward Alston by wearing for dinner a short evening black coat, stick-up collar, and, above all, a made-up tie of most gaudy colours.

It was not only in their dress that some members of the Administration revealed a certain eccentricity. There was the district officer who, when asked what it was he was placing on the luncheon table at Government House replied 'Rhinoceros dung, Sir. I've been looking for it for years.' And how else does one explain how in 1894 John Yule, the only officer at the small and isolated station of Songwe, broke his arm throwing a cricket ball. Again, was it merely inexperience which induced the young official at Fort Anderson to plant his garden with tinned peas?

II

Reginald Maugham has written of Walter Gordon Cumming in the 1890s that 'he was an enormous man, of great personal strength. He was well over six feet in height, and with literally enormous chest and shoulders. He had a strikingly handsome face, with those steely blue eyes which are so characteristically Scottish, his head was crowned by a perfect mane of luxuriant, tawny hair swept back from the forehead and descending to his shoulders behind, where it was gathered into a kind of queue by means of thongs of antelope skin. His hair was surmounted by a wonderful headdress, for a hat I cannot call it, made by himself, and contrived from the hide of a reedbuck which he had shot. His open grey flannel shirt displayed a vast amount of hairy chest and, with his khaki shorts, which he was wont to refer to as his 'copper riveted pants' from the fact that he had reinforced the outer seam with thin copper wire, was all the clothing he wore. His stocking-less feet were thrust into a pair of those South African heelless shoes or sandals known as velt-schoens. Slung over one shoulder, he carried a small silver barrel or keg which he called 'the baby'. It contained about a quart of whisky. In his hand he bore a long staff, and, all in all, I have never seen a more striking or arresting figure. Gordon Cumming had travelled in most parts of the world, though, I imagine, not in the same costume, and his acquaintance with men, things and out-of-the-way places, like Sam Weller's knowledge of London, was 'extensive and peculiar'. Of his appearance, or what people thought of him, he was wholly regardless. The natives were terrified of him; and well they might be, for, to them, at any rate it would be difficult to imagine a more formidable personality, or one whose language, especially when his reserve forces were called into play, was more striking.'

III

Sitting as Second Class Magistrate, a District Commissioner heard a serious case of such gravity that he ordered six strokes of the birch. He knew that the law provided for such punishment for the offence in question, but what he had overlooked was that only First Class Magistrates and judges were permitted to order birchings. When the case record was sent for confirmation by the High Court, he received a letter from the Registrar demanding to know under what authority he had ordered the corporal punishment – which had already been carried out. His reply, clear and precise, was to the effect that it was well known that the District Commissioner was the father and mother of the people in his district, and consequently when passing the sentence he had acted *in loco parentis*.

IV

This was but one example of the sport known to some as 'Registrar baiting' Another is that of the District Commissioner who regularly got fed up with being required to execute distraint warrants and seize the goods of debtor traders, usually Asians, in remote trading centres, who were in default of paying their bills. It was not the justice of the matter that concerned him but the futility in most cases of trying to seize goods from traders skilled through long practice in giving the appearance of destitution. And there seemed to be no end to the warrants sent to him by the Registrar, a man, he was convinced, who knew little, and understood less, about the realities of life outside his no doubt plush and luxuriant office in the High Court. He eventually handled them by letting the trader in question know that he would call on him at a given time and that unless he had cash available to cover at least some of the debt, he would seize a more than adequate quantity of his personal goods. If the trader thought he could empty his house and store of their contents so as to leave nothing to be seized, and return them after the DC's visit, he would be mistaken, for he made it clear that he would bear this trick in mind when next the man's trading licence fell due for renewal. The result of this was that the trader usually had an acceptable amount of cash ready for the officer to call, thereby avoiding any of his property being seized. It was a process well known to, and accepted by, both sides. It enabled the DC to report the outcome to the Registrar in a letter which he always enjoyed drafting: 'I have this day relieved the defendant of the sum of £X, or to be more precise, he relieved himself.'

V

In the days immediately following the declaration of a state of emergency in 1959, the Government was determined to re-assert and to demonstrate its authority. As part of doing this they issued instructions to District Commissioners to tour their districts extensively with platoons of police or the KAR to 'show the flag'. This instruction was passed on to a newly appointed Assistant District Commissioner, who immediately set about the task. On the first day, the DC became somewhat worried that his ADC was very late in returning back to the *boma*. When he asked what had delayed him, the ADC explained that it had taken a very long time to call at each house in the villages he had visited, knock on the door, produce and unfold the Union Flag that he was carrying, and showing it to the baffled occupants.

VI

Many Administrative Officers recalled how impressed they were as newly appointed Cadets with the first District Commissioner under whom they worked. The impression was usually a positive one of sincere admiration for the DC's knowledge, help and guidance. Occasionally, however, the lasting impression was less positive. One such was a new ADC who was obliged to delay his first *ulendo* – to which he was looking forward with excited anticipation – because the DC, an avid cricket fan who had once played for Oundle, spent three whole days sitting in the ADC's new car parked just outside the *boma*, listening to the test match on the car's radio. The ADC was gravely put out but felt that he ought not to complain. His restraint was sorely tested, however, when, at the end of the test match – which, much to the DC's delight, England won by ten wickets – he was able to set out on *ulendo*, only to find that the car battery was flat.

VII

And it wasn't only flat batteries that some ADCs didn't like, for there was one who could not abide flat, or nearly flat, land, at least not land near his house. He became a compulsive and life-long terracer. Indeed he carried his compulsion through his years as ADC and DC, even, we are told, into retirement.

If there was the slightest slope in front of, behind, alongside or within reach of his house this officer would have it terraced. Nor did he confine himself to slightly sloping land, for if there was a steep hillside near his dwelling he would treat it in like manner. His technique was simple. The reluctance of his agricultural colleagues to deploy their skills and divert their equipment to terracing land for cosmetic purposes and to satisfy the whim of a fellow officer, persuaded him to design his own equipment for ensuring that his terraces were on or nearly on the contour.

He placed on a coffee table a twelve inch ruler towards each end of which he inserted a pin, making sure that the pin heads were of equal heights above the ruler. On the ruler itself he placed a small spirit level – one which he used to ensure that the turntable on his HMV record player was level. He also had a six foot length of wood on which he marked a line which was the same distance from the lower end as were the pin heads above the ground. He would bend down, close one eye and align the nearest pin head with that at the other end of the ruler, and the two with the line on the length of wood which was held vertically by a *boma* messenger standing some twenty two yards from him. Twenty two yards was the distance selected because, as he pointed out, this was precisely one eightieth of a mile and exactly the length of a cricket pitch. The relevance of this was never explained. The messenger would be asked to move uphill or downhill until the pinheads and the line coincided. The terraces themselves would then be cut by convicts sentenced - usually by the officer himself - to perform public work.

What, you may legitimately enquire, if there was absolutely no slope on the land at all, if it was perfectly flat? This was so in only one case, and here he dug a huge trench at the right hand side of his garden and carefully constructed terraces leading down into it, using the soil from the trench to increase the height of the land at the left hand side of his garden, and thereby produced an even more remarkable display of his obsession. In the rains, of course, the trench became filled with water but, not to be outdone, he turned it into an ornamental lake.

VIII

The desk of a much experienced District Commissioner bore three trays. In descending order of priority and ascending order of contents, they were prominently marked, 'In', 'Out' and 'LBW'. When asked what the last of these stood for, he would hitch up the old college tie that held up his trousers, clench his teeth and growl, 'Let the buggers wait'.

IX

Eccentricity is deeply embedded in the limericiana of Malawi, and extends beyond the civil service, as the following selected examples illustrate.

None could tell if a man from Chipoka
was dyslexic or jimply a soker.
They were no more clear
when, offered a beer,
he said he preferred Cola Coca.

NYASALAND-MALAWI ANECDOTES

When they created the city of Blantyre
they appointed an energetic Town Crier
but when he proclaimed every morning
a false terrorist warning
they eventually renamed him the Town Liar.

An eccentric old chap from Nthandama
slept in a one leggéd pyjama.
Asked why by his wife, Ruth,
he withheld the full truth
for fear the reason might alarm her.

A strange looking man from Sandama
reckoned his Dad was the great Dalai Lama.
But everyone knew
this couldn't be true
for his Pa was just a crazy old farmer.

A terrifying old man from near Rumphi
was morose and really quite grumpy.
He lived in a cave
where he'd rant and he'd rave
in a manner that made us all jumpy.

An aggressive young man from Nkholombidzo
studied, guess what, yes, the art of jujitsu.
When his wife asked him to show her
he decided to throw her
and without further warning just did so.

ooo ☺ ☻ ooo

HIS GRACE'S EARLY MORNING TEA

Is there no Latin word for tea? Upon my soul, if I had known that I would have left the vulgar stuff alone.

Hilaire Belloc.

During his visit to Nyasaland in the 1950s Lord Fisher, the Archbishop of Canterbury, stayed overnight at the home of one of the leading members of the settler community who was also a church warden. After an enjoyable dinner the Archbishop retired for bed. When asked what time he wished to arise in the morning he said that he hoped the family would follow their normal routine and it was agreed that he would be brought an early morning cup of tea and that they would breakfast at 7.30 a.m. After His Grace had retired, the lady of the house gave the head servant instructions as to what he should do in the morning when he took tea to the visitor's bedroom. He was to knock on the door, say clearly 'My Lord, it is the Boy' and wait for the Archbishop to ask him in. He should then enter, say, 'Good morning, my Lord, here is your tea.' The head servant was excited yet understandably a little nervous. He was up early the next morning, made the tea - from locally grown and processed tea leaves - in the best china tea pot, set it on a small tray with cup, saucer, milk, sugar and a plate with six biscuits on it, and covered the whole with a net cloth embroidered at its edges with small coloured beads which had been made at a nearby mission school. He moved carefully to the visitor's bedroom door and knocked. As he did so, the Archbishop – who was about to start his early morning private prayers, and was still a little sleepy - called out 'Who is it?' and was surprised to hear the nervous reply, 'My Boy, it is the Lord.'

ooo ☺ ☻ ooo

In an earlier period, from the days of the first missionary settlements, men of the cloth and matters ecclesiastical figured prominently in the oral tradition of Malawi flavoured limericks, though only the following have survived intact to the present day:

A learned priest from Likoma
loved reading Cicero, Virgil and Homer,
but he gave his Superior a fright
when he read through one night
and was found the next morn in a coma.

A gardener from Old Livingstonia,
suffered badly from grave melancholia.
Having planted a white lily
he felt awfully silly
when up came a bright red begonia.

In greeting his flock in Malawi
an Anglican priest asked 'How are we?
When he received no reply
he realized with a sigh
he was in the Scots church at Bandawe.

The Archbishop of the Province of Machinga
advertized for a diocesan bell ringer.
A campanologist who applied,
when asked, simply sighed,
'I could ring all your bells with one finger.'

ooo ☺ ☻ ooo

VISITING AFRICA

My father used to say 'Superior people never make long visits.
Marianne Moore.

One of the most enduring - and some considered most endearing - traditions in colonial Nyasaland, as no doubt elsewhere in British African territories, was the quaint custom of 'visiting Africa'. It began in the very early days when European travellers relieved themselves in the bush rather than go to the unnecessary trouble of providing lavatory accommodation inside their tents or other transitory living quarters. As time passed and more permanent residences were built, the need for the al fresco solution lessened, and in many cases, especially when European menfolk brought out their wives to live with them, the need itself, but not the practice, disappeared completely as the *chimbuzi,* the lavatory, became an invariable feature of settlers', missionaries' and officials' houses.

The word *'the'* preceding *chimbuzi'* in the singular is important, partly because it overcomes the difficulty of deciding whether to use the ungainly and linguistically incorrect plural *chimbuzis* or to deploy the correct plural *zimbuzi* and risk getting the prefix wrong. Mainly, however, the term 'the *chimbuzi*' was used because there was normally only a single – and here, sensitive as one might try to be, one can no longer avoid using the inelegant noun – latrine, in each residence. Of course, there was not just one sort of latrine available, for there was a choice between a pit latrine, a sand latrine, a sawdust latrine and a bucket latrine, usually with a surmounting well planed wooden seat to complete what became known among some segments of society as a 'thunder box'. Indeed, uppity donas who demanded of the Public Works Department that a water closet be installed in their house, were occasionally referred to as, for example, 'Thunder Box Thelma'. There was the case, too, of the District Commissioner who had his bucket latrine replaced by a proper water closet only when the Queen Mother visited the country and had lunch at his house.

But to return, as it were, to the matter in hand, that of visiting Africa. Whilst a single lavatory sufficed in most homes on most occasions, it often proved inadequate when one entertained a number of guests who needed, whether truly or by reason of long habit, to go to the loo after dinner. On such occasions it continued to be the practice that while the women used the facilities inside the house to 'powder their noses', the men trooped out onto the lawn to relieve themselves: 'to visit Africa' as the practice soon became known. So convenient - and indeed many found enjoyably relaxing, particularly on a warm moonlit evening - did this post-prandial nocturnal sortie prove to be, that even when there were few or even no guests to join the head of the household, it was indulged in, though the solitariness of having no companions with whom to share the pleasure tended to take the gilt off the gingerbread. No: with companions it was much more meaningful and could take numerous forms and variations on forms. For example, with one's back to the house, and standing on the edge of the top terrace of the front lawn, silent competition became a possibility difficult to resist. Many were mentally transported back to their adolescent school days, and cricketing allusions were frequently the vogue, with unexplained references to slow bowling, daisy-cutters, in-swingers and bouncers, and with general agreement that body-liners, full tosses and yorkers were ungentlemanly and at all costs were to be avoided. The thoughtful, or fussy, hostess discreetly provided a set of small embroidered towels close by the front door with which the less careful or less accomplished of her guests – and as a silent reprimand to them and their less careful and less accomplished companions - could wipe their shoes before returning to the ladies, who in fairness and contrary to present day claims, usually took less time to complete their task than did the men. But then, the men from time to time might be delayed by being attacked by red ants which had a predilection for climbing en masse up the trouser leg of the unwary and preoccupied guests.

But enough of these asides. If the single loo proved inadequate to ordinary householders when entertaining a number of guests, clearly the difficulties were multiplied in the case of very large dinner parties, for example at Government House. And it is from Government House that some of the most revealing accounts of visiting Africa have been handed down to us.

I

The first account is of the evening when the male dinner guests deployed themselves at suitable intervals along the neatly trimmed line where the flower garden gave way to the lawn. They were quietly setting about their business, when the nocturnal peace of the capital was shattered by a loud voice from the first floor balcony as the Governor's wife in high dudgeon bellowed 'Not on my roses, you stupid man.'

II

The second is a matter of logistics. There was a widespread belief, backed by the opinion of the long-serving Director of Agriculture, that urine added beneficial nutrients to the soil, provided that one did not use too much of it. The Governor, proud of his gardens and lawns, and of his many first prizes at the annual horticultural show, was keen to follow this advice. He was blessed, ex officio as it were, with the proceeds of a heavy programme of entertaining, but was concerned that he might be too well blessed. Consequently, in order to avoid an over concentration of the proceeds and to spread their benefits more evenly, he instructed his Aide de Camp, a Major of the Grenadier Guards who had not shone unduly as a regimental officer, to 'see to it'. Logistics had never been the Aide de Camp's forte but having pondered the problem for some time he solved it. Thereafter, each evening when His Excellency was entertaining guests to dinner, as the sun was setting and the shadows were lengthening across the reds and yellows of the garden's roses, zinnias, Barberton daisies and cannas, he was to be seen, attired in his blue and scarlet regimental mess uniform, complete with golden epaulettes and gorgettes, dazzling decorations and silver spurs, on the top terrace of the lawn, prodding a series of small white sticks into the grass at intervals precisely measured with the pace stick of the KAR Regimental Sergeant-Major who accompanied him.

III

The mid 1950s were a period of increased political interest in Nyasaland. The Federation had been imposed by the British Government in 1953 and, partly as a counter balance, it was anticipated that significant constitutional advance in favour of African representation would be granted. When Oliver Lyttelton – later Lord Chandos – the Secretary of State for the Colonies, arrived in the country for talks with the Governor and European, African and Asian political leaders, the interest intensified. It was not surprising, therefore, that there should be consternation when, quite suddenly, Lyttelton left the country several days prematurely and at short notice. Rumour and speculation were rife and, to prevent their spreading, the Governor announced that the Secretary of State had injured himself by stumbling while admiring the view of the moonlit landscape from the balcony outside his bedroom at Government House and had had to leave the country for medical treatment.

What had actually happened was that, either having not been extended – which is unlikely - or having declined an invitation to visit Africa after dinner, the Secretary of State had, not unnaturally, felt the need to visit the bathroom in the very early hours of the morning. Sleepy and unsure of the way to the bathroom, he had strolled out onto the balcony, unfortunately strolled a little too far and fell over the rail onto the floor some ten feet below. He was not badly injured but had he made the customary post prandial visit to Africa he might have avoided injury altogether.

IV

The last account concerns a young Administrative Officer who was seconded as a supernumerary Aide de Camp on occasions when the Governor entertained an unusually large number of dinner guests and particularly when really important visitors were present. One such occasion was the visit of the Archbishop of Canterbury, and the young Administrative Officer was asked to 'look after him'. At the end of dinner – a sumptuous and dazzling affair, beginning with an unusually long grace by the Archbishop during which, to the head cook's fury, the soup cooled a good deal – the Governor's wife asked the ladies to accompany her to the drawing room and on their way to 'powder their noses'. As they left, the men moved up the table to the Governor's end and enjoyed a pleasant twenty minutes or so drinking his port and smoking his cigars – both duty-free. When His Excellency considered that almost sufficient time had been allowed for the powdering of all but the most generously proportioned noses, he invited his male guests to visit Africa with him and, if they wished, take their cigars with them. The purple be-cassocked prelate looked a little puzzled but was put at his ease when the young Aide de Camp discreetly said he would accompany him. They all strolled out onto the front lawn where His Grace quickly discerned what was afoot and bonhomously determined to enjoy the ceremony. It was an evening which the Aide de Camp never forgot and which he frequently recalled with pleasure and pride. He was careful to stand next to, but not too close to, the Archbishop who shortly turned to him and said, 'My dear young man, ah, would you be so very kind as to, ah, hold this, ah, cigar for me; the buttons on this cassock are so, ah, confoundedly unmanageable even with two free hands.'

Shortly after the Archbishop of Canterbury's visit, the young Administrative Officer was posted away from the capital and spent the remainder of his career in rural, and often remote, districts of the country, for many years as a District Commissioner, a job he loved and found deeply fulfilling. Many years later, when he retired from the Colonial Service he bought a bungalow in Bognor Regis and lived there very happily, spending most of his time gardening, reading, collecting stamps and doing *The Times* crossword puzzle. Eventually he had to move into an elderly people's home where, now less mobile, he continued to occupy himself contentedly with his stamp collections, his books and his crossword puzzles. It was while he was pondering three down and two across one morning that a young reporter from the local newspaper came to see him. Over coffee, they talked about his African career in the Colonial Service and about the many changes that had taken place on the continent since he left. When the reporter asked if he had ever returned, had he ever visited Africa since he retired, the old man replied 'Oh, yes. Every night!'

ooo ☺ ☻ ooo

A sad old man from Utale
was born not nearby but *patali*.
When asked *when* he was born
he answered, forlorn,
'Kale, achimwene, kale kale.'

ooo ☺ ☻ ooo

GOVERNORS AND PRIME MINISTERS

Towards the end of the colonial era, as the colonies closely approached independence, they usually had both a governor and a prime minister, each appointed by the Queen, the former on the advice of the British prime minister, who was appointed by the Sovereign as the person most likely to command a majority in the House of Commons, and the latter, the local prime minister, appointed by the Governor as the person most likely to command a majority in the colony's legislature. So, one had an interesting chain of authority. The Sovereign appointed the British prime minister, who advised her on the appointment of the Colonial Governor, who appointed the local prime minister. Since the Sovereign's role was closely confined by conventions which gave her next to no room for personal choice, the most influential person in this chain was the British prime minister despite his or her oft repeated protestations that, of course, it was the Secretary of State for the Colonies and, most importantly, the man on the spot, the Governor, who made the decisions. This was a fiction designed to enable the British prime minister to pass the buck to either his Secretary of State for the Colonies or, more likely, the Colonial Governor. None the less, recognizing the constitutional position that a governor represents the Sovereign, most prime ministers habitually bowed their head when first meeting a governor and on greeting him each morning at breakfast. The relationship between a prime minister and a governor could be interesting. Two very different examples spring to mind. In neither case is it likely that the prime minister followed the traditional courtesy of formally bowing his head to the Governor.

I

Die, my dear Doctor? That's the last thing I shall do.
Palmerston.

In 1939 the Governor of Nyasaland, Sir Harold Kittermaster, was taken ill and was diagnosed to be suffering from appendicitis. His condition became serious and although there were 16 Members and 13 Licentiates of the Royal College of Surgeons on the Nyasaland register of medical practitioners, Sir Harold, or his close advisers, or Lady Kittermaster, decided to call in a well known surgeon from Southern Rhodesia, Godfrey Huggins, who was also Southern Rhodesia's prime minister. Huggins, son of an English stockbroker, had first gone to Southern Rhodesia on a short term agreement as a *locum tenens* but then decided to stay in the country. In doing so he forfeited his chances of a promising academic career in a London hospital. When asked to treat Kittermaster, though slightly surprised and rather busy at the time, he quickly agreed and flew straightaway to Zomba. Here he decided on surgery and carried out the appendectomy before flying back to Salisbury. A day or two later, however, the Governor's condition deteriorated. Senior secretariat officers tried anxiously to find out what the constitutional position would be if the Governor became so incapacitated as to be incapable of governing, and decided that the Chief Secretary should assume the administration of the Protectorate if necessary. Huggins was summoned again and he flew hastily to Zomba but despite his valiant and skilful efforts, he was unable to save his patient. Sir Harold Kittermaster died the following day.

II

'As a matter of fact, we both are, and the only difference between us is that I am trying to be, and you can't help it.'
F E Smith when told by a judge that he was extremely offensive.

The second case of the interaction between governor and prime minister is that of Harold Macmillan's visit, as British prime minister, to

Nyasaland in 1960, shortly after delivering his 'wind of change' speech in Accra, Ghana, and shortly before delivering the recycled and virtually identical version in Cape Town. He stayed overnight at Government House as a guest of the Governor, Sir Robert Armitage, who was the great great grandson of a former prime minister of Britain, Spencer Perceval. The Protectorate was still under a state of emergency and Dr. Banda was still detained in Gwelo prison. Macmillan was pressing for the very early and unconditional release of Dr. Banda and the end of the state of emergency, but Armitage was resisting the pressure because he feared that the country was not yet in a sufficiently stable position for him to end it safely. After a fairly large reception, when only a small group of advisers were present, Macmillan argued strongly for Dr. Banda's release. Armitage resisted and neither gave way. Both were tired and stressed and neither, especially following the reception, was in the best mood for polite conversation and compromise. The Nyasaland officials who were present found Macmillan's behaviour 'rude and gross', while the British officials found Armitage 'deliberately offensive' and 'stubborn to the point of insubordination.' The Governor accused Macmillan of being prepared to risk the lives of people living in Nyasaland for the sake of gaining a few votes in England. 'Governor', objected Macmillan, 'that was a most offensive remark.' 'Prime Minister', retorted Armitage, 'It was intended to be.'

ooo ☺ ☻ ooo

FOUR WEDDINGS

Let us be married! Too long we have tarried:
But what shall we do for a ring?
Edward Lear.

Among the many duties and responsibilities that were placed by statute on District Commissioners was that of being Registrar of Marriages, which incorporated not only the registration of marriages but also the performing of marriage ceremonies. Not many District Commissioners in practice officiated at marriage ceremonies, but almost without exception they longed for the opportunity to do so at some time in their career.

I

One of the longest marriage ceremonies on record took place in one of the more remote stations in the southern province. It was the marriage of a bachelor planter who had been in the country for many years. His bride was a much younger lady, in her late teens, whose late father had been an Indian trader and whose late mother had been an African village lady. The banns of marriage were duly posted on the *boma* notice board and when the great day arrived the District Commissioner - who was nearing the end of his career - dressed himself in his beautifully pressed white uniform with its gold oak leaf gorgettes, ceremonial sword and dangerously tight trousers tied down by a strap running under the instep of his boots, and he carefully pinned on the chest of his tunic his six medals: the MC, MBE and four World War I medals. He arranged for a large vase of crimson cannas to be put on his desk and he delicately placed his white pith helmet, with its gilt royal cipher badge and highly polished chin strap, on the table next to it. At 10.30 a.m., the appointed hour, the bride and groom arrived. She was becomingly attired in a long white dress with a muslin veil over her face and she carried a small, pretty bunch of yellow zinnias mixed with orange marigolds. He wore a slightly crumpled dark suit which by all appearances had not seen the light of day nor had enjoyed the moth-ball freedom of the open air for many a year. There was a large gathering of interested and well-wishing onlookers crowded in and around the District Commissioner's office, and it took some time for him to get them all quiet and as many as possible of them seated, mainly on the floor, since, as with most rural stations, the *boma* was not aflush with chairs.

When all was ready and the head clerk had made sure that, as the law required, all windows and doors were open so that the marriage should bear the imprint of public knowledge, the District Commissioner began the ceremony, standing behind his desk with Volume Three of the Protectorate Ordinances open at the relevant page in front of him. He deliberately adopted a demeanour of official sternish propriety softened by a slight paternal smile. The groom stood upright, smoothing the lapels of his jacket and, looking the District Commissioner straight in the eye, he followed his every word diligently. The bride, on whom most eyes were directed, stood nervously with shyly bowed head and her eyes studiously fixed on the polished concrete floor in front of her. When asked if he took this woman to be his lawful wedded wife the groom, with a rich baritone voice assured them all that he did, announcing clearly for all to hear, 'I do.' When the District Commissioner then turned to the bride and asked 'Do you take this man to be your lawful wedded husband?' there was complete silence. The District Commissioner repeated the question, this time a little more loudly and slowly, but in vain. There was still no reply from the bride who was so nervous that she was unable to utter a word, not even the two short syllables so desperately required of her. The District Commissioner tried again, with the same worrying result.

At a loss as to what to do, he adjourned the proceedings for a while during which time the groom sat with his bride in the corner of the office and tried painstakingly to reassure her, comfort her, steady her nerve and induce her to respond. After a while, he told the District Commissioner they were ready to proceed and they returned to their places in front of the District Commissioner's desk. Relieved, the District Commissioner - now smiling more reassuringly and with no trace of the former mild sternness on his face – gently repeated the all important question, 'Do you take this man to be your lawful wedded husband?' To his dismay, the bride began to tremble and, try as she might, was still unable to speak, much as she wanted desperately to say 'I do' and get the whole thing over and done with.

It was now well past one o'clock and to the District Commissioner's continuing loss as to how to handle the unfortunate situation with which he was faced was added his growing hunger – he had been so preoccupied with arranging the ceremony that he had eaten no breakfast that morning. Consequently he told the couple and the crowd of onlookers that he was adjourning the proceedings and would reconvene at 2.30 p.m. Before going to his house for lunch he had a word with the groom and told him that he really must get his bride to say something, preferably 'I do', or the marriage could not go ahead. The groom was sure that he could bring his bride to oblige, and off the District Commissioner went to eat. His curried tinned sausages did not taste as good as they usually did, for he was too preoccupied to enjoy it, and he thought it unwise to drink the three or four bottles of beer that had always succeeded in making the curry palatable in the past.

Promptly at 2.30 p.m. he returned to the office, and was relieved to see the couple waiting for him, both looking slightly more confident than they had before the District Commissioner had gone off for lunch. But the relief was short lived. The bride was still tongue-tied and her trembles were as bad as ever. Stern words from the District Commissioner and still sterner words from the groom failed to elicit an answer. And so it went on. They broke for tea and half an hour later returned to try again. The District Commissioner privately suggested to the groom that maybe a drop of brandy might loosen the young lady's tongue, but he was quickly reminded that this would not do because she was a Moslem.

To the District Commissioner's fear about the lack of progress was now added the dilemma which he discovered by a glance at the Marriage Ordinance that ceremonies had to be performed during the hours of daylight. What would be the legal position if, having got half the marriage ceremony performed, darkness fell before the second half could be accomplished? Could a person be half married? And if so, were both parties half married or was one married and the other not? And if one was and the other was not, which was which? After all, since the groom had agreed to take the bride as his lawful wedded wife, it could be argued that she was married and he not. On the other hand this seemed unfair since he had done all that was required of him and his bride had not. One can readily imagine the turmoil into which these thoughts threw the poor District Commissioner, and through no fault of his own. At the end of a long and distinguished career, when his long held ambition to conduct a marriage ceremony was at last on the point of being fulfilled, was he about to make a colossal mess of it? Was the CMG to which he might reasonably look forward on retirement to be denied him at the last moment? His desperation increased as the sun dropped closer and closer to the horizon, and he tried to drag one last drop of hope - which sprung eternal in his breast, though with less and less spring as the minutes ticked away - from the fact that at this time of the year the sun seemed to set twice. This was a fascinating and quite beautiful scene which he had watched with pleasure for many years as the sun fell first below the summit of the mountain behind the *boma* to re-emerge a few minutes later on the other side before finally dipping silently and irrevocably below the next mountain slope and darkness became complete.

His conscience now began to trouble him. A morally determined man, he had always waited – anxiously licking his lips – for the sun to set before he started his evening drinks, for as a young man he had it impressed upon him that the surest path to dipsomania was to drink before the sun was below the yardarm of the *boma* flagpole, at which moment the police bugler daily raised his bugle to his lips and blew mightily while the Union flag was lowered. Putting his conscience on one side – placing it temporarily in his waistcoat pocket, as he expressed it - and fighting for time, he sent a message to the Officer in Charge of Police and asked him to delay the bugler's bugling, just this once. The Officer in Charge and the bugler were astonished. In the past the District Commissioner had always been keen that no delay whatsoever should occur in lowering the flag and the bugling to accompany it. None the less they did as they were requested.

In other circumstances it would have been a lovely evening and one which the married couple could remember for the rest of their lives; the sun was dipping towards the mountain summit, the sky was a glorious mixture of fiery golds, reds, yellows and oranges, with light purple clouds dotting the horizon. The cicadas were beginning gently to chirrup, the pigeons were quietly cooing, and on the gentle zephyrean movement of the air the perfume of the bauhinias and Cape honeysuckle flowers was conveyed the most delectable of bouquets.

Yet all this beauty was lost on the DC, who would have been tearing his hair, had he any hair to tear. But, whether this beauty, especially the early evening perfumes, was the cause or not, the bride without warning suddenly looked up, screwed up her pretty little nose, wrinkled her equally pretty little face, and sneezed' 'Atisho', which the ever pragmatic DC swore he heard as 'I do' and promptly pronounced them man and wife.

II

One of the shortest marriages – as opposed to marriage ceremonies – recorded, was that of the Administrative Officer who towards the very end of his first leave met and fell in love with a young lady from the north of England. Not a man to miss his chances in life, and aware that it would be another three year tour before he could reasonably expect a similar opportunity to come his way, he proposed to her and was accepted. This was so perilously close to the end of his leave and his imminent return to Africa, and not wishing to deprive himself - or her - of a honeymoon, he lashed out on a special licence, found a fellow officer who was on leave at the same time to be his best man and the wedding was forthwith held at a London registry office. Ten days later, when the couple returned from their honeymoon, the groom started to pack his trunk, and offered to help her pack hers. 'Where are we going?' asked his slightly surprised bride. 'Why, back to Africa', he replied. It is unclear whether or not, in their unusually brief romance and hastily arranged wedding, he had forgotten to tell her what his profession was and where he plied it or, if he had mentioned it, whether or not she had been listening or had her mind on other things, as may well have been the case. In any event, his bride's reaction was to say, 'If you think I am going to that bloody place you are mistaken!' The next day he boarded the boat for Africa and they never saw or heard from each other again.

III

Our third wedding was not so much a short affair as a truncated affair. Like many of his colleagues, the District Commissioner of a District in the Lower River harboured a secret and deeply held desire to conduct a ceremony under the Marriage Act – a title which the black jacketed and pin stripe trousered legal draftsman of the time in Whitehall had failed to appreciate might cause a certain amount of ribaldry and possibly confusion.

One warm and quiet afternoon, after his siesta, the District Commissioner returned, much refreshed after his rest and a cup of tea, to his office to find a well dressed young Indian couple awaiting him. They were in their early twenties; the man wore a smart light coloured suit and the woman a colourful sari. They were studying the notices on the *boma* notice board. The District Commissioner asked if he could be of assistance. The couple seemed to speak Gujurati, a little Chinyanja and very little English.

The District Commissioner spoke no Gujurati and, since he had spent almost all his career in the Tumbuka speaking areas of the north of the country, very little Chinyanja. None the less, the Indian gentleman politely said something about coming to see the District Commissioner about the notice on the board. Looking at their smart appearance, and with a brief look at the notice board, the District Commissioner quickly concluded that they were the couple whose notice of intended marriage had appeared on the board for the past three weeks. Many other notices had been there much longer and were now curling up at the edges in the intense sunlight: the District Commissioner made a mental note to tidy up the notice board when he had time. But at the moment he had a more important matter to deal with.

Delighted that at long last the opportunity to perform a marriage ceremony had now come his way, he lost no time in rearranging the layout of his office, opening, as the law required, all the doors and windows, and with a fatherly beam asked the young couple to stand in front of his desk. He had dealt with the preliminaries and was about to ask if the man took the woman to be his lawful wedded wife, when the head clerk, a grey haired man of long service and great experience, whose mother tongue was Chinyanja and who had picked up more than a little Gujurati, interrupted him and asked if he could have a word in private. The District Commissioner, correctly thinking it would be unseemly to interrupt a wedding half way through, motioned the head clerk aside and said ‘Later, Mr. Kaliu, a little later, please.’ He picked up his copy of the Marriage Act and was about to continue when the head clerk again interrupted him to ask for a private word. Gravely irritated, but believing that if the head clerk was so bold as to interrupt him twice in the middle of such obviously solemn proceedings, the matter must be an important one, he excused himself and apologized to the young couple before him. He moved outside his office and asked what on earth the head clerk wanted to see him about. ‘Sir’, said the head clerk, ‘am I correct in thinking that you are conducting a marriage ceremony in there?’ ‘Of course I am’, the close-to-exploding District Commissioner almost roared, ‘What the devil do you think I am doing?’ ‘Indeed, Sir’ the head clerk continued, ‘but if that is so, I think you should know that the young couple of whom you are making such a fuss did not come here to have the formality of wedlock bestowed upon them, since they are already married, but have come here today simply to take out a trading licence.’

IV

The earliest Christian marriage in Malawi was in 1861 at Magomero in the Shire Highlands, between present day Blantyre and Zomba, where the first missionaries established their settlement in a meander bend of the

Namadzi river. The following account of the marriage is given to us by the Reverend Henry Rowley in his *Twenty Years in Central Africa*:

'The evil of crowding so many people together on so small a plot of ground as that which we occupied was soon apparent in more ways than one. While they were herded together it was useless to think of improving their moral condition; and as soon as we had got rid of the fear of an attack from the Ajawa, the Bishop resolved to have huts built for our people outside the stockade, and to make an effort at the same time to raise their standard of life. He called them all together, therefore, and having pointed out the ground that was to be built upon, told them that if they lived with us they would have to obey our laws.

'That is good,' was the reply. 'You are our father now, and we are your children. It is for the father to make laws, and for the children to obey them.' 'I am glad to hear that,' said the Bishop. 'So bear in mind that henceforth you men must live by yourselves, and you women by yourselves.' 'Is that so?' rejoined they in great astonishment. 'And is that the custom of your country?' 'No,' said the Bishop, 'it is not; and if any one man wishes to have any one woman for his wife, and she is willing to take him for her husband, we shall not object to that.' 'What! and only one wife?' asked the men. And upon the Bishop replying, 'Only one,' they naturally asked if that was the custom of his country, and wherefore. The Bishop then told them that it was and, because we had God's Word, that our custom was more in accordance with God's Word than theirs, and that we obeyed God's Word because men who did not were not so happy as those who did. He begged them to listen to us, and assured them that if they did, it would be for both their present good and their future welfare.

They discussed this question amongst themselves for some time, and then one answered for all. Said he, 'It is very certain that you are not enemies. No enemy would do as you have done. When the Chakundas (slavers) were taking us away you set us free; when we were naked you clothed us; when we are hungry you give us food; if we are sick you give us medicine. No enemy would do that. You must be friends. And as you know more about God than we do, let it be as you say.' And so it was arranged.

A day or two after this conference a young man came to us while we were at dinner, and sat himself down in front of us without speaking. Said the Bishop, 'What do you want?' Said he, 'I have come to have a little talk with you.' But though he came to talk, it was the very thing he did not do, and that surprised us. Our friends were eloquent talkers; there seemed to be established between their brains and the tips of their tongues a perfect bond of sympathy, so that with them thought and speech were twin-born. But we could not get a word from this man; there was evidently something on his mind which disturbed his spirit and made speech difficult to him. At length the Bishop said, 'Tell us what you want or go away.' Then he, evidently with a great effort, replied, 'I want - I want So-and-so for my wife.' When asked if she wished to have him for a husband, he held down his head and said, 'She says so.' And when he brought her to us she did say so. Then the Bishop, William acting as interpreter, spoke to them very gravely upon the duty of husbands towards their wives and the duty of wives towards their husbands, and made the man promise that he would have no other wife while this one lived, and the woman promise that she would have no other husband; and made them both promise that they would be kind and faithful to each other; and ended by making him solemnly promise that he would never sell her. After this they were told that we regarded them as man and wife, and were shown where the village of the married people was to be, and bidden to build a hut for themselves.

Next day we had several candidates for matrimony. One man, however, brought up a woman about whom he had made a very great mistake indeed; for when she was asked if she was willing to have that man for her husband, she broke out into a torrent of abuse against him, and declared that she was not. He went away greatly angered, but in the course of the day, in order to prove to us, I believe, that he was not such an undesirable fellow after all, he came back with two women, both of whom were anxious to be wedded to him.

After this, marriages became popular, until all the men were provided for. Unfortunately we had more women than men, and quarrels as a consequence occasionally took place. The wives began to value their prerogative, and would not quietly permit any other woman to share in their husband's affections, although up to this time they had been accustomed to the arrangements of polygamy. In the end, however, these people lived happily in their new condition, and as a rule they were kind and faithful to one another.

ooo ☺ ☻ ooo

FOUR FUNERALS

I

We have already seen how Sir Harold Kittermaster died in 1939 while still in office. His sudden illness and death naturally caused much agitation in the secretariat where it was unclear at what point the Chief Secretary should take over the administration of the Protectorate as Acting

Governor. The constitution provided for such a take over if, *inter alia*, the Governor became incapacitated either physically or mentally, a provision originally designed to cater for occasions on which a governor became insane. In the history of the British Empire there are fewer of these than one might expect. Though very ill, Sir Harold was still entirely *compos mentis* and able to receive advice and give directions. When he actually died he was still in office and the situation then became clear: the Chief Secretary automatically and immediately became the Acting Governor. There remained, however, the task of arranging Sir Harold's funeral.

No previous governor – certainly not in Nyasaland nor, it was thought at the time, elsewhere – had died in office, so there were none of the precedents on which civil servants so gratefully rely. The well oiled brains of the secretariat machine swung into action and within hours the funeral had been arranged.

A gun carriage was provided by the KAR and hastily repaired by the Public Works Department. The First Battalion was drilled and rehearsed on the 1910 pattern for the memorial service of King Edward VII, the documentation having been discovered in a box that had survived the 1919 destruction by fire of the secretariat building. Incidentally - and leaving aside the much discussed question of what an Assistant Secretary and a stenographer were doing on the evening in question in the basement of the secretariat, other, if anything, than smoking the cigarette that it was believed caused the conflagration – this was not the only colonial secretariat fire that destroyed vast quantities of records. There was a similar fire in Nairobi during Sir Robert Armitage's time there in 1939 – the result of the Deputy Financial Secretary late at night making himself a cup of tea with an electric kettle which he forgot to switch off. A fag or a cuppa: one took one's choice, though if the former included a stenographer one might consider the choices not to be equally balanced. To many, in Nyasaland, in Kenya and elsewhere, the loss of files was a merciful delivery providing the very best of excuses for taking, or not taking, official action.

On the day following His Excellency's death, the funeral cortege set off down hill from Government House, led by the band of the KAR with muffled drums. Behind the band came the freshly green painted gun carriage bearing the Governor's coffin, 'pulled' by white-washed ropes, in front by six, and behind by sixteen, askari. Behind these askari came the most senior civil servants, and finally the remainder of the KAR battalion, marching in slow time and with rifles reversed. It was a solemn, fitting and impressive ceremony, watched by crowds of all races lining the road down from Government House past the Gymkhana Club. From this point onwards there are great uncertainties about, and many versions of, what happened.

Memories fade and differ, but probably the most interesting version is that shortly after the cortege passed the Club one of the sixteen soldiers behind the gun carriage slipped - it was a hot day and an emotional occasion - and his colleagues lost their grip on the ropes with which they were, not pulling, but holding back, the carriage as it moved heavily down the hill. Sensing that all was not well, the six askari in front of the carriage, and the bandsmen in front of them automatically wheeled outwards, and only just in time as the gun carriage, now out of control, gathered speed, trailing behind it the remnants of the askari unit desperately trying to hang on and retrieve some control and sense of decorum. They failed, and the carriage rumbled past the District Commissioner's office near the foot of the hill, where still more people had gathered to pay their last respects, and across the main road where it ploughed through the low brick wall surrounding the cemetery and came to a blessed halt. The military officers and civil officials in a most commendable fashion soon regained their composure, and the funeral service was conducted with great solemnity and reverence. From a tragic situation they had restored the dignity that the occasion demanded.

There are many who dispute this account of events. Only one man, then a very young army officer, who was present, is still alive and he can not be drawn on the subject. He does point out, however, two things. First, in the wall surrounding the cemetery, there is an irregularity in the brick bonding and a difference in the colour of the bricks where the gate used to be rather than where it is now, directly opposite the road down from Government House. Secondly, the first grave one sees on entering the cemetery, immediately inside the present gateway, a little oddly, is Sir Harold Kittermaster's.

II

This is no time for making new enemies.
Voltaire, on his deathbed.

Our second funeral was quite different. It was that of a former District Commissioner whose father had been a well known big game hunter towards the end of the nineteenth century. The DC served the country with distinction and for many years. When the time came for him to retire he decided not to return to England – which he had not visited for many years – but to live on in Nyasaland. Indeed, he already had a home there which he had set up with his long standing partner, an African lady whom he had met as a young administrative officer. Their home was by the lake shore and it was a remarkable dwelling, furnished with beautiful locally made furniture with each wall of its many rooms lined from floor to ceiling with book cases sagging under the weight of the complete sets of Wisden and the Encyclopaedia Britannica, lovely leather bound copies of the Greek and Latin classics and others dealing with big game hunting, military history and opera. Where there were gaps that were too small for book shelves, the walls bore faded photographs of his ancestors and of his public school.

Few people visited the couple, who were totally content with their own company, but they always welcomed most warmly those visitors who did call on them. These included the current District Commissioner who much admired the old man and his record and who deeply enjoyed hearing stories of his early days in the country, now several decades past. His visitors did *not* include any of the clergy from the nearby Anglican Mission. Why was this? It was because in the eyes of the clergy, the old DC was, and had been for many years, 'living in sin'. This view held by men of the cloth disturbed neither the old man nor his partner, for, as we have said, they were content with their own company.

Came the day when the old chap died, the current DC visited the Mission and asked if a member of the clergy would conduct the funeral ceremony for interment at the mission cemetery. He was astounded by their reply. Under no circumstances would they contemplate conducting the service and it was utterly out of the question that such a man should be buried in their consecrated grounds, because, as the DC well knew - and had done nothing about it - the man had been 'living in sin'. The DC's astonishment turned quickly to fury. The, as he saw it, sanctimonious attitude of the missionaries, was beyond belief. What was more, they were insulting the memory of a man who had served the country faithfully, loyally and with great distinction, and in the course of his long career had been the author of many acts, both officially and as matters of personal charity, to the undoubted benefit of the African population of the districts in which he served or lived in retirement. Indisposed, and too angry, to argue with the missionaries, the DC turned on his heel, returned to the *boma*, ordered that the flag be lowered to half mast and determined to give the dead man what he described as 'the best bloody funeral this country has ever seen.'

The following morning, the whole complement of police officers, dressed in their number one uniforms and led by the officer in charge, arrived at the old DC's house, and on their shoulders they carried his body in a coffin draped with the Union flag and topped with his Military Cross and dress sword, in a slow march to the little used municipal grave yard, a tiny plot of ground near the *boma*, in which were interred the remains of the few Europeans who had died there. The DC, reasoning that if he were permitted to conduct marriage services, there was no reason why he should not conduct a funeral service. Consequently, attired in his white and specially starched dress uniform with its gold oak leaf gorgettes and a broad black armband, his Wolesley helmet on his head – held high and defiantly - and his leather mosquito boots beneath his tight trousers anchored down by straps under the instep, he walked gravely behind the coffin to the cemetery. Here he stood at the head of the grave, with the widowed partner at his side, and delivered a resounding eulogy in which he loudly – he hoped loudly enough to be heard at the mission – and proudly recounted the deceased's many acts of public service, valour and charity, accompanied by an occasional snide, but probably well deserved, aside on the local Anglican clergy. As the coffin was lowered into the ground, the DC and the officer in charge of police pulled their ceremonial swords from their scabbards and gave a flourishing salute, while the police bugler sounded the Last Post and four policemen on each side of the grave raised their rifles and fired shots into the still air. The District Commissioner had fulfilled his promise to give the old man 'the best bloody funeral this country has even seen.'

III

The evil that men do lives after them,
the good is oft interred with their bones.
Shakespeare, Julius Caesar.

Malawi's first State Funeral, and by far its best funeral ever attended, was that of the country's first, and only, prime minister and its first president. It was seen by many as marking the end of an era. A senior diplomat's report on the death and funeral of Dr. Banda in 1999 read:

'Following the death of Dr. Hastings Kamuzu Banda, the Ngwazi or Conqueror as he was known, in the Garden City Clinic in Johannesburg on 25 November, a tripartite committee was formed consisting of the ruling party, the United Democratic Front (UDF), the Malawi Congress Party (MCP) - Dr. Banda's party - and the family to decide the funeral arrangements. Out of respect to the former founder of present day Malawi, the Committee decided to stage a State Funeral on 3 December. Despite the hostility between the UDF and MCP, there was, for once, considerable multi-party unity in honouring the former President.

After embalming and the search for an appropriate gold-plated casket, which had to be imported from the USA, Dr Banda's corpse was returned first to Blantyre for a lying-in ceremony and then on to New State House in Lilongwe on Monday 1 December. The President was still indisposed and the Vice President was despatched to meet the body in Blantyre. The crowds at the Chileka airport were such that the police lost control and it was reported in the press that 40 people were injured in the stampede to view the coffin's arrival. A day or so later in Lilongwe I witnessed the arrival of the cortege, which was at least three miles long and, for most of it, took up two lanes of road. Bare-footed villagers lined the road from the airport and visibly showed their respect by singing mournful-type hymns as the hearse, a converted Toyota pick-up, passed by. In the meantime, a hired JCB was digging and bricklayers shoring up the 6 metre deep grave in central Lilongwe, set back 100 yards from the main highway and next to the war memorial. Plans have been announced to create a mausoleum above the grave and install an electrical device to raise and lower the casket for viewing. The contractors have said that the lid of the coffin will also open and close. The area has been designated 'Hero's Acre'.

The funeral was split into two halves. The first half was held at New State House in Lilongwe for invited guests. My wife and I arrived for the ceremony and were shown into New State House where we assumed the ceremony was being held, to find ourselves placed in front of the open casket, amongst grieving relatives. After about half an hour, we were told politely to move round to the back of the palace because President Mugabe, Joshua Nkhomo and President Masire of Botswana were due to arrive to pay their last respects. Unfortunately, the foreign guests were two hours late in arriving and the crowds at New State House, manageable at first, swelled to around 20,000 when the ceremony in the gardens started at around 12.30. Shade and seating was minimal. There was, however, a poignant moment when the casket arrived in the gardens from the House and the heavens opened with thunder and lightning and a sudden downpour of rain. The majority of the crowd remained at attention, many with plastic chairs on their heads to protect them from the rain. There was genuine respect and sorrow. A number of people fainted, from a mixture of heat and emotion.

The tripartite committee theme dominated the ceremony with President Muluzi delivering a respectful eulogy praising Dr. Banda's statesmanship in accepting change, defeat in the 1994 elections and his public apology in 1995. MCP President Gwanda Chakuamba gave an emotional address highlighting the Doctor's major achievements, establishing Lilongwe as the capital city, setting up the University of Malawi, two North-South roads and unity amongst the 50 or so tribes in the country, and repeating Dr. Banda's simple vision - that Malawians must have enough food to eat, decent clothing and houses that do not leak. After leaving New State House the cortege drove slowly to the gravesite, to the sound of a sombre 19 gun salute, where 250,000 people had gathered for the final ceremony.

There were some sporadic scuffles by occasional dissenters, which the police sorted out quickly, and an errant green snake which was quickly despatched. Overall, the event was reverent, and the crowds were well-behaved and sorrowful. There was one incident which lightened the day; the casket had just been lowered into the grave and a few minutes later a hand, followed by an arm appeared over the parapet of the grave. You can imagine the wide eyes of the onlookers. All was later revealed as five soldiers emerged from the pit. They had been sent down earlier to receive and position the casket. Shock quickly turned to smiles. On behalf of my Government I laid a wreath at the gravesite.'

IV

The first Christian funerals in Malawi were at Magomero in 1861. In the evening of 14 August a small boy aged about six years was so very ill that a few minutes after Bishop Mackenzie baptized him – the first Christian baptism in the country – he died and was shortly buried. A month later two baby girls died; both were very sick and one of them rolled onto a kitchen fire and was badly burned. Both soon died. They, too, were baptized and buried at Magomero. At five o'clock in the afternoon of 31 January 1862 the Bishop himself died, near Chiromo. Though he died in what later became Portuguese East Africa, his body was immediately taken across the river into present day Malawi and was buried there. By the time he was interred it was already too dark for the Rev. Burrup, who was with him, to read the burial service, so he said all that he could remember of it.

ooo ☺ ☻ ooo

CONTRASTING PENAL SYSTEMS

I

NYASALAND: MIKUYU

Mikuyu in recent years has become best known as the prison in which those who ran foul of the Banda regime were incarcerated during much of the first republic. But Mikuyu has a much longer and altogether more congenial past. Ironically, the account that is about to be given lies in the African-detested decade of the Federation of the Rhodesias and Nyasaland, 1953-1963. During that period Mikuyu was a federal administered prison farm.

A visitor to the farm in the late 1950s noted and was impressed by the neatly kept flower beds, the whitewashed stones lining the well swept paths and roadways, the neat thatch on the buildings and the general air of smartness. He was met at the gate by a Malawian warder in crisply laundered khaki uniform with a green band round his felt bush hat and green gorgettes on his collar. The gate keeper showed him the way to the Superintendent's office where he was warmly welcomed by the officer in charge, Mr. Knee, known to all – including the inmates privately – as 'Knocker'. The visitor sat down in the chair in front of the Superintendent's beautifully polished and paper-free desk, accepted the mug of tea offered to him, and told Knocker how impressed he was with the appearance of what he had seen of the farm on his way from the gate. He also remarked that the prison service made the best mugs of tea he had ever had the pleasure of drinking; indeed the Mikuyu tea closely rivalled that which he had enjoyed at the Central Prison only the day before, made for him by the assistant hangman. Knocker thanked him and asked if he would like to tour the rest of the premises. The visitor was delighted and said how much he would enjoy it. Knocker asked if he would mind being shown around by one of his colleagues since he had to finish off an important report which was already a few days late. His visitor did not mind at all.

The Superintendent rang a bell placed at the side of his desk and when a sergeant warder entered - with a resounding stamping of his dazzlingly polished boots and a guardsman-like salute - he asked him if he would be kind enough to ask Mr. Rupert to join them. Shortly there was a knock on the door and a man quietly entered. He was in his fifties, small and wiry of build, tanned and wearing an immaculately starched and pressed khaki shirt and shorts - rather shorter than his Superintendent's. There were no insignia on his shirt and he wore no hat so the visitor was unable to guess his rank. Knocker introduced them and said that Rupert would show the visitor round the farm. Wherever they walked Rupert exchanged a cheery word with the prisoners and received a smiling greeting in return. He was clearly extremely proud of the work being done, the food crops and vegetables being grown, the sisal that was used to make rope and matting, the tradesmen's workshops - carpentry, bricklaying, tin-smithing and tailoring – and the small dam that had been built to provide water for irrigating the vegetable gardens. The visitor remarked that all this must involve Rupert in a great deal of work. Rupert agreed and with a sad sigh said that he was soon to leave Mikuyu and he really did not know how Knocker would manage since there was no one to succeed him.

Eventually they returned to the Superintendent's office, Rupert shook the visitor's hand warmly, said how much he had enjoyed showing him their work, and left. The visitor talked for a while and congratulated

Knocker on the excellent work that was being done and the general air of efficiency and progress that was evident throughout his tour of the premises. He added that the Superintendent was fortunate in having such an enthusiastic and competent colleague as he had in Rupert. Knocker agreed and said he relied on him a good deal. He pushed the half-written report he was writing wearily to one side, and added that he would have liked to give the job of writing it to Rupert, who would make a much better job of it, but felt it would not be fair on him with all his other work. 'I understand he is about to leave Mikuyu', said the visitor, 'You will miss him a good deal.' 'Yes', replied the Superintendent, 'We don't often have white prisoners here and Rupert's sentence is up in a fortnight's time.'

II

MOZAMBIQUE: VILLA GAMITTO

In the early 1960s District Commissioners in charge of the Nyasaland districts which shared a border with Mozambique were encouraged by their superiors to pay courtesy calls on their Portuguese counterparts, partly in a spirit of good neighbourliness and partly for gathering military and political intelligence as to their activities and intentions. In those cases where there were significant Portuguese settlements fairly close to the border regular contact between the administrators of the two countries was common, but in others, especially in the more remote areas, contact was spasmodic and infrequent. In one of the Nyasaland districts of the Central Province there had been no contact with the Administrador at Villa Gamito across the border for several years. Now, however, an early visit became important.

The Nyasaland DC looked forward to the visit and made what arrangements he could to visit Villa Gamito, few as they were. He discovered that there had been a road of sorts made many years earlier between his district and the Portuguese settlement and that this might still be passable in a Land Rover. Early one morning at the beginning of the dry season, just before day break, the DC set off in his Land Rover accompanied by his sergeant messenger. They journeyed quite easily to the District boundary and then carried on along the track which quickly became overgrown, through countryside that was very sparsely populated. Indeed they passed hardly any villages and those that they did pass were very small and seemed totally abandoned. Several times they lost the track and had to walk round in circles until eventually they found it again.

On their way the sergeant messenger spoke of the dislike the Nyasaland Africans generally had for the Portuguese mainly because of the stories they heard of brutal treatment meted out through the medium of the *palmatoria*, a wooden instrument in the shape of a perforated table tennis bat used to beat the hands, and the *bastinado*, a stick which they applied vigorously to the soles of the feet of those they arrested. The District Commissioner voiced his disapproval of these alleged practices and the conversation turned to other matters until the sergeant messenger dozed off.

The sergeant woke up, rubbed his eyes and straightened his tunic as they neared a small settlement of permanent houses – Villa Gamito. They drove up to the white painted building from which the Portuguese national flag fluttered. The sergeant stayed in the vehicle while the DC went to the front door of the building and asked in Chinyanja to see the Administrador. Shortly the Administrador appeared, smiling and extending his hand to greet his British visitor. He was youngish, perhaps in his early thirties, short of stature and tanned of complexion. He asked the DC to enter the building and there he offered him a glass of whisky, it being his understanding that all British males drank whisky on every possible occasion, even, as was the case on this visit, at 10.30 a.m. Judging it easier to accept than to explain that the Administrador's understanding of British drinking habits contained some inaccuracies, the DC thanked him and took a few sips from the large glass offered to him.

The Administrador showed his guest round the station, which because of its smallness did not detain them long, and then invited him to lunch at his house. Here, he met the Administrador's young and pretty wife and their small, curly haired, one year old child. Their house was large and immaculately kept but the DC could not help noticing that there were firearms – rifles and shotguns – leaning against the walls of each room that he entered. He was fascinated, too, by the small, quite tiny, pistol that his host had tucked into the waistband of his trousers. The lunch of piri-piri chicken, exquisitely prepared and presented, was accompanied by several glasses of Mateus Rosé wine. After lunch the Administrador suggested that they adjourn to his office to exchange information and views. Since he would be leaving straight from the office to return to Nyasaland, the DC thanked and took his leave of the Administrador's wife. She hoped he would come again soon and that he would bring his own wife with him; she was the only white woman on the station.

The two administrators walked to the office where, partly because neither spoke more than a few words of the other's language and partly because of the post-prandial timing, their conversation was soon in danger of petering out. To keep it going the DC asked about the local wage rates and was told that they depended on the work being done. 'Well, how much do you pay that man out there cutting the grass?' pointing to an elderly man rather lethargically swinging a curved piece of metal at the grass outside the office. 'Nothing', came the reply. 'Why is that?' the District Commissioner further enquired, not because he thought the slow rate at which the grass was being cut merited a substantial reward but he did think it deserved some remuneration. 'Oh, he's a prisoner', the Administrador explained. 'What's he been convicted of?' asked the DC, trying to wring as much conversation out of the subject as he could. 'Murder', replied his host. Surprised at this answer, the DC asked, 'Do you not have capital punishment for murder in Mozambique?' 'Oh, yes, we hang murderers.' 'Well, when are you going to hang him?' 'When he's finished cutting the grass.'

ooo ☺ ☻ ooo

A Peace Corps volunteer in Malawi
asked me to tell him the *nthawi*.
My answer was crisp,
though I speak with a lisp:
'I haven't a watch, I am sowi.'

ooo ☺ ☻ ooo

WATCHMEN

Sed quis custodiet ipsos custodes?

I

The Retail Shop Workers Wages Advisory Board, despite the elegant prolixity of its title and the distinction of its members – a District Commissioner, who was the chairman, a chief and a minister of religion – attracted little public attention, largely because it had little to do. It was supposed to meet four times a year, but often it had no business to discuss and on such occasions the members readily accepted the Secretary's advice that they need not meet. There was, however, one matter that occupied their attention and caused them a good deal of trouble. It concerned the statutory minimum remuneration to be paid to night watchmen at retail shops.

It was universally recognized and not disputed that these night watchmen simply arrived at the premises just before nightfall, carrying a blanket and a knobkerrie, made a shelter of cardboard boxes across the doorstep, chatted with neighbouring colleagues, smoked one last cigarette of the day, then – often a few hours later - crawled into their cardboard refuge and went to sleep. In the morning at dawn – known locally as 'bird belch', or some such expression – they woke up, exited from their cardboard boxes, rolled up their blanket, picked up their knobkerrie and left for home. On only one day a month did this routine vary: they did not go straight home but waited for their employer's arrival in order to receive their pay. Largely as a result of this regime, watchmen had always been paid the same as unskilled labourers, and even this struck some of the less liberal employers as being too generous. Now, however, with growing trade union intervention and threats of industrial action - a term that seemed to some less appropriate than industrial inaction - the Commissioner for Labour asked the Retail Shop Workers Wages Advisory Board to consider afresh the minimum wages that should be paid to the watchmen.

The members of the Board listened carefully to the trade union representative, who argued that the watchmen were not simply the equivalent of unskilled workers, but carried heavy responsibilities and were exposed nightly to the danger of attack from would-be burglars and other villains. If these dangers were not real, why did the employers not simply leave their premises unguarded? The Senior Labour Officer, who was also present, as an adviser, countered by pointing out that no attack on a watchman had been reported for many years and in fact, far from being in a dangerous position, the watchmen were perfectly safe in their cardboard shelters. He conceded that they did carry heavier responsibilities than did ordinary unskilled labourers but this was counterbalanced by the physically undemanding nature of their task, carried out in the cool of night as compared with unskilled labouring in the heat of the day. The members of the Board agreed to ponder these points in private. They did not like equally balanced arguments but preferred clearer cut cases which made their job of adjudication so much easier.

The Senior Labour Officer then suggested that the Board might like to reach a decision on the basis of how many hours the watchmen worked as compared with those of labourers. He pointed out that from the time they entered their boxes to the time they exited them their daily number of hours worked was much the same as those of labourers. In any case, it was not reasonable to include the time taken in setting up and dismantling the shelters, smoking *fodya* and chatting with friends. The clandestine counting of fingers and thumbs beneath the table at which the Board was sitting as members tried to calculate whether or not this was accurate, was soon interrupted by the trade union official proclaiming that he clearly remembered that on the visit a few years earlier made by no less a person than the Secretary of State for the Colonies, a Welshman, the Colonial Secretary had told a number of trade union officials that for decades the South Wales coal miners had included 'washing up' time in the pit head baths as part of their working hours, and no one nowadays challenged this. The chief confirmed this assertion, adding that he had himself undertaken a British Council study tour of the Welsh valleys and had witnessed the miners emerging from the pits, much, he felt, like the watchmen emerging from their cardboard boxes. The parallel was clear. The minister of religion was impressed by the analogy being drawn. The District Commissioner was significantly less impressed. The members agreed to consider this point also in private.

Being on what seemed to him to be the winning side at the moment, the trade union official further invoked the name of the Secretary of State who during his visit had mentioned to him the concept of 'unsocial hours' hitherto unknown in Nyasaland. There could be no clearer case of unsocial hours than that of the retail shop night watchmen who, for the sake of a better word, worked from dusk to dawn. The chief whispered to the District Commissioner that so far as he was concerned – and he expected so far as the DC was concerned – his own social hours coincided precisely with the dusk to dawn period. He was not prepared, however, openly to challenge the claim being made by the trade union official. Once more the Board decided to discuss the point in camera.

Emboldened by the lack of challenge to his unsocial hours point, the trade union official pushed his case further. Whereas labourers had provided for them at the employer's expense all that they needed in the way of equipment for carrying out the job – hoes, shovels, pangas, etc. – the night watchmen were obliged to provide their own materials. 'What materials?' the astonished Senior Labour Officer enquired. 'Why, their blankets, knobkerries and cardboard boxes', replied the official, his face bearing the pain of a man who could not understand why a civil servant of the Senior Labour Officer's status should not immediately grasp this point. Not just any old box would suffice. It had to be as sturdy, water proof and wind proof as possible. Such worthy boxes were not easy to come by and were much in demand. Furthermore, they had to be stored secretly during the hours of daylight – not always an easy matter. They could not just leave them on the premises since there they would quickly be nicked; you know how vulnerable premises and materials are when there is no watchman present! The chief and the minister busied themselves with relating the various types of cardboard box which they had seen in different places over the years. As to their merits, the minister felt that Lux soap powder boxes had much to commend them while the chief thought that Sunlight soap boxes and Tom Tom cartons in which were packed the country's best selling packets of fags both had the edge on Lux. The Chairman could get no indication from their faces as to whether or not they thought the particular point about watchmen providing their own shelters, whether boxes of Lux or of Sunlight soap or of Tom Tom cigarettes, had merit in it. Fast becoming exhausted, he said that this point would be added to those that they would discuss in private. His main fear was that the Senior Labour Officer, already puce of complexion, would turn apoplectic and this might lead to an adjournment and the repetition of the whole proceeding, a prospect he most earnestly desired to avoid.

The last point to be raised by the trade union official was potentially the most difficult of them all, but, miraculously, it contained the seeds whereby the whole question of the appropriate level of wages to be paid to retail shop watchmen was to be resolved. The point concerned the payment of time and a half or double time wage rates which virtually all employees in the country were paid if they worked on public holidays. The difficulty was that whereas other employees would not normally be expected to work on public holidays and to do so would naturally involve them in extra work, the night watchmen clearly were expected to work on public holidays. It was precisely when others were not working that the services of the watchmen were most needed. But, the union official argued, even if this were accepted, it did not cater for the fact that the watchmen guarded the premises not only at night but also, on public holidays, during the day. At this point, the exasperated Senior Labour Officer lifted his arms and covered his face with the damp palms of his hands, burying his throbbing head in them. He was too tired to continue the fight. The trade union official beamed and magnanimously told the Board – to their undoubted relief - that he had no more points that he wished to raise, and perhaps the members could now reach a decision.

The Board, under the weary Chairman's guidance, did not take nearly so long to reach a judgment as they had feared. There were a number of points on which they were conscious that they had not reached a decision during the meeting: the comparison of watchmen with unskilled labourers; the number of hours worked, whatever 'worked' meant in this case; the similarity, or otherwise, of miners' 'washing up' time and the nightly construction of cardboard shelters; the unsocial hours aspect of night watchmen's work; and the provision of 'specialised equipment', albeit cardboard boxes, blankets and knobkerries, by the watchmen. All these points had been challenged and remained undecided. The only point that had not been challenged – almost exclusively because everyone except the trade union official was too tired to take it up – was the question of the appropriate hourly rate of pay for working on public holidays. It was here, by replacing logic with the prospect of relief from their misery, that the Board found its escape route. They reserved for subsequent discussion all contested and undecided points at some unspecified time in the future, should this – as they fervently hoped would not be the case - prove necessary, and ruled that retail shop watchmen should be paid double the normal rate for working on public holidays.

Only the Senior Labour Officer left dissatisfied, but even he was relieved that the whole matter was, he hoped, over and done with. The chief and the minister of religion left the board room arm in arm, delighting in their continued personal recollections of the immense and fascinating variety of night shelters they had come across over the years, and the ingenuity – 'astonishing inventiveness' according to the minister, and 'native genius' according to the chief – displayed by the watchmen in constructing such a great variety of refuges. The trade union official had won a major victory over the forces of capitalist repression and parsimony, and as he left he chanced a knowing wink at the District Commissioner and was gratified to observe in return a wink from the District Commissioner – or was it a nervous twitch?

II

Late in the afternoon of his first day at his new station, a small sub-*boma*, the Assistant District Commissioner was preparing to leave the office and return to his house for a bath and a drink before his evening meal. He had put the few files back in the filing cupboard – a hand-made piece of furniture constructed from the wooden boxes in which tins of petrol were at that time purchased – he had checked that the safe was securely locked and that he had the key safely in the pocket of his shorts, and he was having a last look round the office when he heard a gentle knock on the open door. He turned round and saw standing before him a small man, no taller than five feet in his stocking feet - not that he wore stockings or indeed footwear of any sort – very slim in build, with a mischievous wrinkled face and a happy smile. He had only one arm - his left - and under it he carried a rolled up mat and a blanket. He wore a khaki shirt and shorts, and on his head was a battered red fez with a regimental badge on the front of it. He placed the mat and blanket on the floor, stood as rigidly to attention as his spare frame and absence of one arm permitted, saluted with his left hand and said, 'Good afternoon, *Bwana*.' The ADC returned the greeting and enquired, 'Who are you?' 'Sah', came the reply accompanied by another salute, 'I am Usi, your *boma* night watchman.'

'Come in', invited the ADC, and Usi entered. The ADC sat down but Usi insisted on remaining standing. The ADC asked about the regimental cap badge and was told that it was the cap badge of the Somali Camel Corps: Usi had acquired it when he fought in Somaliland with the KAR in the early 1900s. 'Is that where you lost your arm?' 'No, Sah, I lost it in East Africa during the First World War when I was hit by a piece of German shrapnel.'

The ADC asked how long Usi had been a watchman and was told, 'Many years, Sah. You see, I am one of the most famous of all *boma* watchmen and I enjoy a great reputation throughout the whole of the country, not only as a former soldier, but as a night watchman.' The ADC was surprised by this claim, as Usi could see by his raised eyebrow and the general look on his face. 'Sah. You think I am not of an appropriate stature and strength to be such a good night watchman?' 'Well', said the ADC, 'I am a little surprised. After all, you do not have the build of a prize fighter.' 'You are quite right, *Bwana*', Usi responded, 'But I fear that you do not fully understand the nature of my task nor how I go about it, nor do you appreciate that as a young man in the KAR I was exceptionally fit and agile.' The ADC indicated that he would like to learn more, so Usi continued. 'It is true that I do not have the build of a pugilist but before the First World War I was three times the KAR one hundred yard sprint champion. No one could outclass or even match me. My task here at your *boma,* Sah, is not, as you seem to suppose, forcefully to ward off any felonious intruders, but to deploy my ability as a sprinter. If I hear anyone trying to break into the *boma* at night I do not confront them – that would be a very foolish thing for me to do – but instead I run like the wind to the *boma* lines and tell the messengers of the intrusion. They then run with me – usually a little behind me – back to the *boma*, where they, and not I, tackle the intruders.'

III

In February 1959, just before the state of emergency was declared, there was a good deal of general jitteriness among all sections of the community, many people fearing an outbreak of violence and a repressive response from the security forces. At this time there occurred a brutal murder which, had it become public knowledge, would seriously have increased the jitteriness. For this reason the authorities, and particularly the police, were keen to apprehend the murderer as soon as possible. The case was finally solved and the murderer arrested about a week later.

The murder took place at a 'canteen', owned by an absentee Indian landlord and managed by an African storekeeper, and was located only a few miles from Zomba. Early on the morning in question, the storekeeper arrived at the canteen and was horrified to discover the headless body of the night watchman lying across the door of the building in exactly the same place as he normally slept. He had been decapitated while he was still asleep. The terrified storekeeper told his teenage son to run as fast as he could to Zomba and tell the police what had happened.

Some two hours later a police team of detectives arrived, questioned the storekeeper and others nearby, and took measurements, photographs and fingerprints. At noon, the Detective Inspector in charge of the investigations was surprised by the arrival of the Deputy Commissioner of Police who was keen to encourage his officers to get a move on and waste no time in solving the case. This irritated the Inspector because he was working as fast and effectively as he could and did not see that the Deputy Commissioner's intervention was likely to help.

The Deputy Commissioner checked on each step that the investigating team had made and looked as if he was about to take over the investigation himself. He asked what areas had been finger printed and photographed and he pointed to a bloody handprint, complete with finger and palm prints, on the whitewashed wall next to the door near where the headless body of the unfortunate watchman was lying. Sarcastically, he asked, 'Inspector, I suppose you missed that hand print?' 'No, Sir, I did not miss it.' 'And you have photographed it and taken finger prints?' 'No, Sir, I have not.' On hearing this utterly unexpected reply, the astonished Deputy Commissioner could scarcely believe his ears. 'Why the devil not, man?' he exploded. He was relieved, however, when the Inspector replied, 'Because I already know whose palm print it is.' 'And do you know where the owner of the palm print is right now?' 'Yes, Sir, he is sitting in the back of that Land Rover over there, with a number of my officers.'

Believing that the case had been wrapped up in record time, and already beginning mentally to draft his report which would give the impression that he had personally played a leading part in solving the crime, he turned to the Inspector, clapped him on the back and said, 'Good fellow. Well done. Splendid effort.' Almost as an afterthought, he added, 'By the way, is the man known to us?' 'Yes, Sir, he is well known to both of us.' The Deputy Commissioner was further delighted: he had always advocated the early use of criminal records and the study of 'form' as steps towards discovering who might have committed various crimes; indeed he was known to the Malawian policemen as *Bwana Forumi*. 'Who is he?' asked the Deputy Commissioner as he mentally flicked through a list of hardened recidivists for whose incarceration he had been responsible as a younger officer. 'Well, Sir,' said the Inspector, not being quite sure where the conversation was leading him and the Deputy Commissioner, 'he is my Detective Sergeant.' The Deputy Commissioner was aghast. 'Are you sure?'

'Quite sure, Sir.' 'Do you mean to tell me that one of our police officers is a murderer?' 'Good Heavens, no, Sir. He was carrying the decapitated head to the Land Rover for forensic examination when he slipped and had to steady himself by reaching out for the wall of the canteen. His hands, not unnaturally, were covered in blood and that is how his palm print came to be on the wall next to the doorway.'

IV

The District Commissioner returned from a week's *ulendo* exhausted. Whereas he usually slept in a tent, on this occasion he stayed in a rest house. He was keen to make an early start each day before it became too hot, and he instructed the rest house watchman to wake him promptly and precisely at half past five each morning. The watchman - who like most others possessed no watch - was so nervous lest he be late in waking the DC that twice every night for six nights he woke him to ask the time.

V

In one of the Districts in which we lived we were the only European couple. We were by no means lonely for we had each other and we had a gramophone with which we enjoyed listening to operas in the evenings. One of those we particularly enjoyed was Verdi's *Rigoletto*. Our enjoyment was, however, interrupted each time we played it by the watchman - who, like all *alonda* slept on the *khonde* - in the closing stages of the opera, knocking on the sitting room door and shouting, '*Bwana*?' Yet when I asked him what he wanted he replied, 'I thought you called me.' This happened on several occasions and eventually we ignored the knocking on the door until the music was finished – only a short time. Always his explanation was that he thought I had called him. The matter was a great puzzle to us until, following the libretto rather more closely than formerly, we discovered that in the very final scene, as Rigoletto is handed a sack, which he supposed contained the Duke's body, he revengefully cried out loudly, 'Chuck him in the water' – in Italian, 'All'onda! All'onda!'

ooo ☺ ☻ ooo

A painter from the PWD
looked at the walls, then said to me,
'I know you like pink
but white is better, I think,
And I'm sure on reflection you'll agree.'

GUVNA'METRICS

There are three kinds of lies: lies, damned lies and statistics.
Disraeli.

If one had wanted to join the ranks of the governors of Nyasaland, how ought one to have gone about it? Some guidance may be found in the little known science of Guvna'metrics, the use of statistics and other data to analyse governors and governorships.

For the ambitious with an eye on the gleaming portals of Government House, education was important, but only to the extent that one should have gone to a public school. Yet it was equally important not to be scholarly or to have academic pretensions. Only half the governors of Nyasaland went to university and only two of them got a second class honours degree, while the rest got thirds. Taking colonial governors in Africa as a whole, three-quarters of them got seconds and only one sixth got thirds. Nyasaland, it appears, got more than its fair share of third class graduates - which is not the same as third class governors. In later life, a number of them collected papers with the intention of writing their memoirs. Indeed, a few purloined so many official files that it's a wonder they weren't locked up for it. Sir Harry Johnston, the first governor - although he carried the title of Commissioner and Consul-General - published many books, including his autobiography. Sir Hubert Young, the seventh governor, wrote two and Sir Alfred Sharpe, the second governor, wrote one. None of the others published anything, save possibly for a brief outline account of their stewardship in the Journal of the Royal Africa Society, when they retired.

It was essential also, preferably fairly early on in one's career, to find oneself a wife, desirably a good looking one though some seem to have fallen at least marginally short in this respect. All the governors, when appointed to Nyasaland, other than Johnston and Sir William Manning, the third governor, were married. Without a wife the governors would themselves have had to open numerous flower shows, adjudicate at baby competitions and judge art exhibitions. They would also have had to turn elsewhere to find a Chief Commissioner of the Girl Guides and local President of the Red Cross Society, and someone else to measure out the sugar to the head cook at Government House each day - and carefully lock the door afterwards.

Having found oneself a wife, it was important for the aspiring governor to have children. Save for Johnston, all the governors had children, often two, three or four and - in the case of Sir Charles Bowring, the sixth governor, who married later in life and may have felt that he had already wasted enough time - seven children: four sons and three daughters. Of course, one need not go quite that far, but a couple seemed to help. In any case they didn't disturb one's life too much, because they were normally packed off to school overseas – usually 'at home' or in 'the old country' - at about the age of six, and when the daughters returned from finishing school in Switzerland they would hopefully be wise enough to avoid the advances of dashing, sun-tanned, young army officers - or less athletic but more cunning Assistant District Commissioners. It was the case, however, that one of the governors felt obliged to call out the duty company of the KAR to scour the slopes of Zomba Mountain to flush out his daughter and the subaltern with whom she was spending the afternoon studying, she told her father, nature.

Contrary to popular belief, it was not necessary for the aspiring governor to go out of his way to become a member of one of the more prestigious London clubs. Only two, Sir Edmund Richards, the tenth governor, and Sir Glyn Jones, the thirteenth and last governor, were members of the Athenaeum. And only two, Sir Thomas Shenton Thomas, the sixth governor, and Jones again, were members of the MCC. The rest didn't seem to bother, and many listed no clubs at all in *Who's Who*.

On the other hand, seven of the eight governors of Nyasaland who listed any recreations in *Who's Who* named golf. Of the remainder, while Johnston listed painting, music and biology, none of the others listed any recreations. On the whole, however, golf could be important, both in its own right and in other contexts shortly to be suggested.

Next, if one wanted to become governor one should arrange to get oneself made a Commander of the Order of St. Michael and St. George. This was the crucial decoration. The MBEs early on mattered little – and one had to assess whether it was better to accept what little was offered early on in one's career or risk waiting for something more substantial later on - but the CMG was indispensable. Every single one of those who went to Nyasaland after Manning, was so decorated, well in advance of becoming governor. On being elevated to gubernatorial office, all of them were created KCMG, and four of them were later created GCMG. But the CMG - to the disrespectful, 'Call me God', or in Colby's case, 'Cotton, Maize and Groundnuts' - the CMG had to come first.

Closely connected to the acquisition of a CMG was the post one occupied immediately before becoming governor. That is to say, the office of Chief Secretary. Nine of the ten governors of Nyasaland who were career colonial administrators were elevated directly from a Chief Secretaryship or a closely equivalent office. Being made a Chief Secretary was an important penultimate step on the road, up past the *boma* and the Gymkhana Club, to the wrought iron gates of Government House. If, however, one wished to risk not becoming a Chief Secretary, there was an alternative: being a Provincial Commissioner in the remotest possible province from

Government House and the secretariat. There, one could rule without interference from the centre and thereby build up for oneself an enviable reputation which was more likely to be accepted than checked on. This was not as difficult a task as might be supposed. Sir Harold Kittermaster, the eighth governor of Nyasaland, Sir Vincent Glenday and Sir Gerald Reece moved from the Northern Frontier Province of Kenya to become governors of Somaliland; Sir Richard Turnbull moved from the same Kenya post to become governor of Tanganyika; Sir Glyn Jones moved from Barotseland in Northern Rhodesia to become governor of Nyasaland; and Sir Cosmo Haskard moved from the Northern Province of Nyasaland to become governor of the Falkland Islands.

Having been to a public school and having sedulously avoided distinction at university; having married and having had children; having saved the expenditure on membership of London clubs and having indulged in a little golf; having acquired a CMG and having become a Chief Secretary or a Provincial Commissioner of some out of the way province, and finally having become Governor, one might find that one quite liked the job and wished to acquire further governorships. If this were one's ambition, it was a good thing to have been a soldier, to have stayed in Nyasaland for a very short time and to have some connection with Wales. All three of these qualifications were necessary. Manning was commissioned in the South Wales Borderers, lasted only a little over two years in Nyasaland and accumulated four governorships before he retired. Young, the other soldier-governor, was born in Wrexham, stayed only twenty-two months in Nyasaland and became governor of three colonies before he retired. None of the others was a soldier, none stayed for so short a period and only two others, Thomas and Kittermaster, were governors of three colonies.

For the ambitious governor-to-be, it didn't matter what one's father's profession was, though it was probably safer to be the son of a parson or a general. But one should so contrive to be conceived that one was born in the northern summer. Half the Nyasaland governors were conceived in August, September or October – probably on leave and as the autumn evenings began to get chilly - and were born in May, June or July. Only two - the last two - were born in deep winter, one just before Christmas and the other just after. Despite the application of rigorous analytical techniques, Guvna'metrics has so far failed to unearth a convincing causal connection between cold weather conception and the end of empire.

It is unclear which, and how many, Christian names the infant prospective governor ought to be given when baptized. Three were named Henry and three were named Charles. One of them had both these regal names. As for how many, two governors had a single name, eight had two, two had three names and one, Sir Henry Charles Donald Cleveland

Mackenzie-Kennedy, the ninth governor, had four - or five, if one uncouples his hyphenated Scottish surname. It may be significant that those two governors with three Christian names - and neither of them included Henry or Charles - were in that very small group of the most dynamic of all Nyasaland governors, whereas he with four Christian names, which included both Henry and Charles, was among the least successful. As a broad guide to parents and god-parents, Guvna'metrics suggests two principles. First, the names Henry and Charles are best avoided, and a combination of both could be disastrous. Second, bestowing one Christian name is OK, two is risky - might be good, might be bad - three is very good, and four should not under any circumstances be contemplated.

On the other hand, if one turns from the beginning - conception, birth and baptism - to the later years of one's life, and if one wished to draw one's pension for a protracted period, as one might, it was best to have become governor at the very beginning or at the very end of the colonial era. The first two and the last two governors averaged 27 years in retirement, whereas the rest averaged only nine years. The low point was in the middle: Sir Hubert Young drew his pension for only five years, and poor Kittermaster, the only governor to die in office, did not live long enough to draw it at all. Even more important in the later years of one's life, it was prudent to book oneself into the nearest BUPA hospital and stay there, preferably in intensive care, or at the very least in a high dependency unit, for the whole of December and January each year and again in June. Ten of the thirteen governors - well over three-quarters of them - passed away during those three months. They seemed pretty safe for the rest of the year, and none died in the six months covering spring and autumn, during which seasons the KAR askari on guard at the pearly gates, ready for a final presentation of arms, could safely stand down - though not too far down. The expenditure on BUPA care would readily be recovered by drawing one's pension for a longer period - almost certainly until the following June or December.

Physical height was also important, not so much *per se* but as a guide to when, during the colonial era, one ought to make one's bid to be appointed governor – to make one's attempt on the summit, as it were. The evidence is clear. Johnston the first and Jones the last governor of Nyasaland, were both vertically challenged, that is to say they were men of limited stature. Kittermaster, appointed at the half way point of Nyasaland's colonial history, was immensely tall – already six feet seven inches before he left school. The point being made is reinforced by closer Guvna'metric examination: of the last three governors, Colby was taller than Armitage and Armitage was taller than Jones. Manifestly, if one was tall, one's assault on the oxygen-rare heights of pro-consular office should not have been made at the beginning or the end of the Protectorate's existence, and conversely, if one were short, the 1930s in ultimate career terms were, one might say, a time to lie low.

There are a number of important implications of this question of gubernatorial stature during the second half of the colonial era. First, many governors reaching the end of their career sought to supplement their pension by selling their ceremonial uniform to their successors. So long as succeeding governors got shorter this was not a problem because it simply involved chopping a few inches off the trouser legs. The question of one's sword dragging on the ground was a more difficult, but not insuperable, problem. There was, however, a particular danger in having governors of decreasing size. Both Colby and Jones suffered a blackout in the bathroom at Government House. Colby was not in too much danger, but Jones was. Having slipped down into the water, he was lucky that his wife was able to pull him out before he drowned. It was fortunate in this respect that whilst the governors got smaller their wives got bigger. This is an intriguing question on which some of our most outstanding Guvna'metricians and analysts are currently working. Most important of all, it may be that the diminishing size of governors was a powerful factor in the process of decolonization: no metropolitan power could be expected to go on indefinitely finding ever shorter candidates.

This, then, seems to be the sort of advice, based on rigorous Guvna'metric analysis, that could have proved helpful to young officers yearning to become governor of Nyasaland. But, for the passionately determined, other steps might have helped. For example, one could contrive to play golf at times when it was known His Excellency would also be playing. It was a risky tactic. Whilst it would bring one to the attention of the Governor, one needed to play sufficiently well to impress him, but poorly enough not to eclipse him. As in the case of visiting Africa after dinner, it was safer to position oneself a little distance from the Governor but within, shall we say, seeing distance. Again, whilst publicly praising the virtues of district life in remote areas - 'close to Africa, old chap' - one could take clandestine steps to have oneself posted to the secretariat as soon as possible - 'at the centre of things, old boy'. No district officer was ever appointed governor of Nyasaland without having first served in a secretariat. Or one could have a wife who was prominent in the Guides, Red Cross or Garden Club, and who regularly gave coffee mornings at which she demurely, modestly and obliquely mentioned the diligence and brilliance of her husband. This, too, was a dangerous tactic, but possibly worth trying if one were truly keen on becoming governor. The question of signing the Government House book was a tricky one. It was important to do so occasionally, even if one got a friend - a visiting resident magistrate or a public works supervisor who happened to be passing through, for example - to forge one's signature, as a means of drawing His Excellency's attention to one's existence. But it should not be overdone, lest he conclude that one was spending too much time wandering around Zomba with little else to do but sign books. Judicious signing of the book could lead to receiving a coveted invitation to drinks, or even dinner, at Government House, where one - or one's pretty little wife - could attempt to talk a lot of sound sense when chatting with the Governor.

It is regrettable that the science of Guvna'metrics has emerged largely post-colonially, when but a handful of tiny dependencies still sport the office of governor, when even the Sovereign's representatives there are seldom knighted, and when, one might say, the horse has bolted. On the other hand, had the techniques been available in colonial times to guide aspirants in their careers, the numbers panting at the doors of Government House, and calling at the Colonial Office on leave – 'Just happened to be passing, Sir, so I thought I'd pop in to say hello' - would have caused a problem. Faced with such numbers the Colonial Office would have been tempted to fall back on less well known criteria for selecting governors, including, possibly, merit. As it was, there were so many officers in the Colonial Service of outstanding merit that it was often difficult to choose between a number of well deserving candidates, and consequently the Colonial Office had to use other criteria for selecting men for the topmost position. It is these criteria that Guvna'metrics has uncovered for us.

ooo ☺ ☻ ooo

THE INTERPRETERS

It is not simply the nuances that may be lost in translations.
Sometimes the whole damned sense disappears.

Anon.

I

When being taught about the interpretation of statutes, traditional court chairmen were encouraged to turn first to the interpretation section of the statute in question, next to the General Interpretation Ordinance, and, if these failed, to consult a reputable dictionary.

In answer to an examination question on the Game Ordinance, one of the chairmen defined the word 'trophy' as 'haemorrhoids, suffered in wartime.' Deeply puzzled by this astonishing answer, the examiner spent several days trying to work out how the chairman had come upon this extraordinary definition. After much painstaking research, he discovered in the dictionary that the word 'trophies' was therein defined as 'weapons seized in battle from the vanquished and placed in piles for distribution to the victors'.

II

It was the general practice that when Administrative Officers addressed public meetings they used an interpreter even when, as was usually the case, they were perfectly capable of delivering their address in the local language. Some of the less experienced interpreters were, on occasion, prone to misinterpretation either because they did not know the meaning of the words used or because they did not fully grasp the accent of the Administrative Officer for whom they were interpreting. This very rarely happened but when it did it was capable of worrying, but more often amusing, distortions.

There was, for example, the meeting at which the District Commissioner was encouraging villagers to pay very close attention to what he was about to say. When he paused after introducing his speech with the words 'Now, you must all pay attention to what I am saying' he was disturbed to hear the interpreter translate what he had said by using the words 'Now you must all pay ten shillings for what I am about to tell you.' The faces of the villagers sitting on the ground in front of him showed not the slightest sign of surprise or concern at this apparent extortion – it was far too hot for them to be paying attention, let alone ten shillings.

III

At another village meeting the District Commissioner was answering questions put to him by those present. The villagers were concerned that so many of their young men emigrated to work on the farms and mines of southern African countries, frequently without making adequate provision for their wives and families. At the very least, they complained, these young men came back with undesirable habits and at worst they did not come back at all. How were they to dissuade their young men from leaving home in this way?

The DC, trying to capitalize on the question, explained that in his view the young men left because their home villages did not offer sufficient earning opportunities or rewards to retain them. If only they would grow the cash crops – cotton, groundnuts and surplus maize - that the Government was constantly going on about, the village economies would improve, there would be greater wealth locally and young men would be less inclined to go to South Africa or Southern Rhodesia. The solution was in their hands, here in the cultivation of their own land: 'My advice is basically for you all to make your land more attractive.'

The DC was satisfied with the soundness of this advice, but he was significantly less satisfied with the translation of his young interpreter who conveyed his message with words, 'You must all cultivate your land with a tractor.' Visions drifted across his mind of huge red Massey Harris tractors imminently trundling over the horizon, descending on the terrified villagers and overnight replacing the short-handled hoes which were the only implements available in the area. Although one old man, experienced through long habit in feigning agreement with District Commissioners, gently clapped his hands and quietly muttered '*Indithu, Bwana*', for the rest of his audience, already nodding off in the heat, no such visions, or indeed any visions, were crossing their minds.

IV

It was very rare indeed for a District Commissioner to need to deliver a reprimand to a chief, and on those rare occasions when it was necessary, he usually decided, things having got to this stage, that there was little point in his pulling his punches and that his message must be conveyed in forthright terms. To ensure that the message was accurately conveyed and to bring as much dignity to the occasion as possible, he also used his most senior African colleague, the head clerk - invariably a man of advancing years and great experience - to interpret for him.

In one such case, the chief - one of the leading chiefs in the country - was a well educated man, who had enjoyed a remarkable number of quite lengthy British Council study tours of England. As a result his grasp of the English language was excellent. Similarly, the DC's fluency in Chinyanja was remarkable: probably the best in the country. Consequently, neither the chief nor the DC needed an interpreter. None the less, to mark the importance and formality of the occasion, the DC asked that his head clerk should interpret for him. The chief agreed. The head clerk was also fluent in both English and Chinyanja and he was well known for his diplomatic skills. None of them - the chief, the DC and the head clerk – looked forward to the reprimand, but each of them decided to make the best of an unhappy job.

The task was made less daunting by the head clerk, without in any way altering the sense of what the District Commissioner was saying, deploying in Chinyanja less robust terms than the Commissioner used in English. But the chief also played his part in making the occasion bearable. At one point, after the head clerk had interpreted a passage, the chief gently raised his hand, and with a mildly pained expression on his otherwise emotionless face - save for a twinkle in his eye - said, addressing the head clerk, 'Please excuse me, my friend. I assure you that I have no wish to criticize, especially on such an important occasion as this, but when the *Bwana* DC uses a word such as "outrageous", are you sure that "less than helpful" conveys the same meaning? And when he says that he firmly has it in mind slashing my salary and suspending me from my chiefdomship, ought you really to interpret these words as "might have to reconsider my position as a chief?" Turning then to the DC, he concluded, 'Please continue.'

V

There is only one known case of the Government Board of Examiners over-ruling a decision of one of their senior language examiners. The circumstances were that the examiner in question suffered from a rather severe stammer. This caused few problems until one particular oral examination in Chinyanja, when he came face to face with a young candidate who, unknown to him, had an equally serious stammer. The examiner lengthily stuttered his opening question and the candidate with agonizing prolixity stuttered his reply. The examiner considered this a brazen impertinence, and warned the candidate that the examination was a serious matter that could affect his future progress in the service. The wretched officer smiled weakly and nodded his agreement, and the examination continued – but not for long. After two or three further syncopated questions and staccato replies, the examiner had had enough, told the candidate to get out and failed him, a decision that was immediately overturned on appeal to the Board, whose Chairman knew of the candidate's speech impediment but had failed to tell the examiner.

VI

Some years ago there was a brief but none the less serious period of alarm caused by a local newspaper article reporting an outbreak of anthrax in the country. The report was unclear in some respects, for example as to where the outbreak was occurring, and as to whether the disease was attacking animals, in which case it would kill off large numbers of both domestic and wild creatures, or whether it was attacking humans in which case it would resemble serious pneumonia and might well also be fatal. The government veterinary and medical health authorities were both puzzled and deeply concerned. They had received no reports of the trouble save from the newspaper report. They made enquiries of their field staff, who were unable to throw any light on the matter, and eventually they were obliged to quiz the novice reporter who had written the article.

The reporter, imagining himself already a Fleet Street worthy, initially adamantly refused to help, arguing that journalists never revealed their sources. Eventually, however, when the seriousness of the situation was impressed upon him, he told them where the information had come from: a junior clerk in the DC's office in a tobacco growing district of the Central Province. Urgently, the veterinary and medical officers telephoned the DC and told him of the report and the source of information.

The DC summoned the clerk to explain what had happened. The young man, who hoped one day to be referred to in the press as 'Our Mponela social affairs correspondent', said that, as interesting events cropped up, he sent a brief account to the journalist in Blantyre. He never got paid for these items, and lived in hope of fame rather than fortune. He explained that a week earlier he had been asked to accompany the ADC on *ulendo*, and just as they were about to leave the *boma*, the veterinary officer had asked if, in the course of any meetings held, the ADC would be so kind as to warn villagers about a disease, anthra something or other. The ADC had never heard of it but agreed to mention the matter at his meetings. He asked the veterinary officer if he would jot down a few notes on the subject, which he hurriedly did. Incidentally, it was this veterinary officer who first defined the role of DCs and ADCs as getting out into the villages, meeting the people, talking to them, finding out what they were doing and telling them to stop it.

In due course the ADC held his meetings and spoke of the disease as the vet had asked him. Translating for the ADC was a difficult task because some of the words were technical and the clerk had the nagging feeling that the ADC understood rather less than he was giving the impression he did. Even so, all went well; the village audiences nodded politely, asked no questions and said '*Inde, Bwana*' at the appropriate points.

The clerk decided to write a piece for his journalist friend. Fortunately, he had retrieved the note that the veterinary officer had scribbled for the ADC and found that the important word, the name of the disease, had been abbreviated to 'anthra'. Fortunately, too, he could remember most – though it was not much – of what the ADC had said at the meetings. He turned next to his battered and dog-eared school dictionary to see if that trusty tome could throw light on the disease in question. He was not disappointed, and there at the top of the left hand page at which the dictionary opened was the very word: anthrax! Even better in the eyes of this budding reporter was the definition: 'in animals fatal acute septicaemia, in humans a serious form of pneumonia.'

He explained all this to the DC, who asked to see the veterinary officer's note and the clerk's dictionary. After a little thumbing through the dictionary at arms length - only partly because he was short sighted - he found the page starting with 'anthrax'. A thorough man, he gently turned to the preceding page and there at the foot were the words, 'anthracnose: a fungal disease in plants.'

VII

A young police officer and an air hostess with whom he had struck up a friendship, spent a happy day by the Mpatamanga Falls on the Shire River. When, on their way back to Blantyre, he said to her, 'How about a spot of *chakudya* when we get back?' she replied, 'Yes, that would be very nice, but can we have something to eat first?'

VIII

Officials at the Foreign Office were most deeply disturbed by a letter from Sir Harry Johnston in the early 1890s to the effect that, in the course of operations on Lake Nyasa, he had seized, and was holding hostage, a 'dau' of the Sultan of Zanzibar. Interpreting this to mean that he had seized and was detaining one of the Sultan's daughters, they immediately demanded that the daughter be released and that Johnston should give a full explanation of his outrageous actions. They had not yet become fully acquainted with Johnston's pedantic spelling but were much relieved when he told them that 'dau' was the correct spelling of the word 'dhow', an Arab boat.

IX

In August 1861, Bishop Mackenzie, arrived in the Shire Highlands to set up a UMCA mission station and help to bring about the end of the slave trade. At a meeting on his arrival he made his purpose known to the chiefs and their people and asked them solemnly to promise that they would not buy or sell men, women and children again. It was important to get their agreement. He recorded their reply: 'After some moments of silence, a deep "Aye" came from the assembly.' Immediately accepting this response, the good bishop may have been taking a risk, for, rather than the response being the English 'Aye' meaning 'Yes' it could easily have been the Chicewa 'Ai', meaning 'No'.

JULIUS

Lux in tenebris

Julius was one of those men whose face is a necessity rather than an adornment. This did not worry him because, as he pointed out, although he felt sorry for those who had to look at it, he stood behind it and had over the years got used to it and rather liked it. His nose had a disconcerting bend in it half way down. His mouth seemed to have rather more teeth than those of most people, and they were long, discoloured - '*fodya, Bwana*' - and overlapped. Yet, like him, one did become used to it and there was something likable about it, for his eyes radiated enthusiasm and humour. By profession he was a wood carver. Not just any old wood, but *mpingu*, ebony. He lived in a village in an area, dry and searing in summer and humid in the wet season, an area where *mpingu* grew, though it took a specialist like Julius to find it. He seemed to know where every *mpingu* tree was growing and kept this knowledge to himself except that, to divert attention, he would occasionally show others where one of the inferior specimens was growing. He carved the black wood into spears, walking sticks, animals – elephants, hippos, rhinos, buffalos – and birds, especially fish eagles and owls. These were well done but he took little pride in them. His delight was in the cigarette boxes he made. There were boxes with intricately carved lids but he derived the greatest joy from those with plain lids, whose surface he polished until they shone and when tilted revealed the beautiful grain. The surfaces of no other *mpingu* worker in the whole country showed this grain as did Julius's. Such was his pride that he did not sell the very best of these astonishingly beautiful pieces of work but kept them for his occasional visitor to admire and for he himself to enjoy as every day he took each one of them gently from the soft cloth in which he wrapped them, looked at them lovingly and gave them a gentle buffing.

But Julius's *mpingu* boxes were not the only things in which he took great pride. Over the years he developed a remarkable technique for bringing any conversation with selected acquaintances round to the subject of electric lighting. He might start off on the remotest of topics but in the end he would steer it to electric lighting. When this point was reached he would say, 'Would you like to visit my house? It has electric light, you know.' This, of course, caused the astonishment Julius intended and so much enjoyed, for everyone knew that the nearest electricity was at least twenty miles away. How could one decline this remarkable invitation to visit Julius's house and see his electric light? When one reached his village – which like so many villages in the country was *pafupi pang'ono,* a little bit nearby – one was taken to an unremarkable mud and grass hut, slightly more in need of maintenance than its neighbours, and asked to wait a moment or two so that Julius could turn on the electricity. Shortly, one was invited in and there indeed, glowing from a point above his tin trunk containing his precious ebony boxes, was hanging an electric light bulb. From the glass bulb he had removed the metal holder and replaced it with a home-made cork. Through this cork he had pushed a length of string the lower end of which was immersed in the paraffin that filled the bulb, and the upper end of which was gently burning.

ooo ☺ ☻ ooo

ASSESSING THE LIABILITY TO PAY POLL TAX

But in this world nothing can be said to be certain, except death and taxes.
Benjamin Franklin.

Under the African Tax Ordinance in Nyasaland all African males over the apparent age of eighteen years who had, or had the ability to find, the means of paying were liable to pay poll tax. Assessing this liability fell to members of the District Administration. Normally this presented no difficulties for it was usually quite apparent from the appearance of the person brought before the District Commissioner or Assistant District Commissioner that they were African and were male. More difficult on some occasions was the assessment of age. The law specified ‘apparent age’, so DCs and ADCs could usually argue, if challenged, that the person in question appeared to *them* to be of or over the age of eighteen years. On occasions, however, there were problems.

There were a number of rules of thumb to determine whether a young man standing in front of one was eighteen. One could ask him or his village headman or relative when he was born in terms of whether it was before, at or after a well known event, for example a flood or a famine, or who the DC was at the time. This worked well and reaching a conclusion was not difficult.

Another rule of thumb – although that was not the word he used – was that of a long-serving and much respected Police Officer who swore that the least fallible method of determining whether a male was over or under eighteen years was to ask him to turn sideways and briefly study his bodily profile. If his buttocks curved outwards then the person was under eighteen years of age. If they did not so curve outwards then the person was over the age of eighteen years. Having checked the officer's sanity and been completely reassured by his most senior colleagues, and having surreptitiously studied the next few candidates to appear before him, one DC concluded that there was a degree of validity in the method, but that it was too broad brush a technique to be reliable, that the margin of error was too great, and that it was a potentially dangerous system. He feared that asking those charged with tax default to turn sideways in court while he lowered his eyes to examine their profile would reinforce their view that the British were no longer sufficiently sane to continue ruling them. But he long hoped that he might be invited to an eighteenth birthday party to witness, secretly, any sudden change of profile that might take place, though - the moment of metamorphosis being uncertain - he doubted if he would have the nerve or determination to keep his eyes on anyone's profile for a full twenty-four hours.

Fortunately, one did not have to rely on the technique of this Police Officer. *Boma* messengers, particularly the really good 'uns, men with records of hundreds of tax defaulter arrests to their credit, provided the best rule of thumb – or, more accurately, rule of arm – method of determining age. They asked the young African concerned to lift his right arm, take it across the top of his head and see how far his fingers reached down the left cheek of his face. If the finger tips reached the bottom edge of his lower jaw bone he was at least eighteen years of age. If not, he wasn't. The advice of these wise, pragmatic messengers was that there was no better way of determining age, at least not in a hurry. And, in retirement, having done their limited early morning exercises, many former administrative officers still to this day look intently in the shaving mirror, gently stretch their arms over their balding heads, reach down as far as they can and mutter quietly to themselves, 'There now, that's not too bad. I'm not as old as I look.'

Others were not satisfied with rules of thumb. The High Court usually and wisely studiously avoided having anything to do with tax default cases; there were too many of them and they did not have the glamour and awful responsibilities of murder, manslaughter, grievous bodily harm, arson and larceny. There came the time, however, when a case of tax default was challenged and taken on appeal to the High Court. The Chief Justice himself reviewed the case and went to immense pains to see that the law was meticulously followed and that justice was done. He called for expert medical advice – that of the Chief Medical Officer – and ruled that in cases of doubt as to age, the person charged was to have his elbow x-rayed and this would tell conclusively whether or not the age of eighteen years had been reached. This struck most Administrative Officers as being at the very least eccentric and certainly unrealistic. The further DCs and ADCs were posted from the urban centres, hospitals and the High Court, the more eccentric and unrealistic the Chief Justice's ruling seemed. Several officers, in their capacity as magistrates, decided that perhaps x-raying the elbow was but a refinement of the messengers' rule of arm technique. Some felt that if a senior officer - from whichever department, judicial or medical - was intent on making a fool of himself it was their duty to assist him to do so, so they began to send dozens of young Africans charged with tax default to be examined at the nearest hospital that possessed an x-ray machine,. Hospitals with x-ray machines were often many miles distant from the *boma*, and their machines were already fully used with what the doctors saw, no doubt correctly, as more deserving cases. They were disinclined to move stooping and wheezing elderly people, and young mothers carrying sick children, out of the queue and have their place taken by strapping young teenagers. Inevitably, as the number of requests to have these young men examined increased to worrying proportions, the medical officers complained to the Chief Medical Officer. When he in turn tried to do something about it he was reminded of his own expert advice to the Chief Justice and to his lordship's ruling based on that advice. Prompted by the Provincial Commissioner, the Chief Medical Officer invited the Chief Justice and his wife to an unusually sumptuous private dinner party. Over port the Chief Medical Officer enquired after the Chief Justice's family's health and when told that it was good, he casually remarked that he was pleased about this because the hospital staff were hard pressed examining the elbows of potential tax defaulters sent to them by the DCs. The following morning the Chief Justice called for the record of a further case of tax default, and modified his earlier ruling: x-rays should be used only if other methods of determining age seemed to the DC to be unreliable. He did not specify what these other methods might be and no one thought it necessary to tell him about the length of tax payers' arms, still less the curvature of their dorsal profile.

None of these methods of assessing age was proof against 'substitution'. A young ADC was sitting in his office one morning when in strode an elegant but rather haughty European woman smartly dressed in riding breeches and carrying a riding crop. 'Why', she demanded without introduction, 'have you convicted my stable boy and sentenced him to a month's penal labour?' The ADC was not conscious of knowing either the woman or her stable boy, but it turned out that among the dozen or so tax cases he had heard the previous day was this be-jodhpurred lady's stable boy and he had indeed sentenced him to a month's penal labour. When he asked why she was disputing this conviction she asked if he had seen the person concerned and did he know how old he was? The ADC replied that of course he had seen him - even on a very busy morning one occasionally lifted one's eyes from the record book to look at the accused - but he did not know his precise age. 'Well', she proceeded, 'he's twelve!' Clearly, at such a young age, neither the flexible arm nor the dorsal profile test would have been necessary, but he could not believe that he had ignored the obvious youth of a twelve year old. The woman manifestly did not intend to leave his office until the matter was settled to her satisfaction. The ADC asked where her stable boy was now and she said 'Outside your office. I brought him here to prove that he is nowhere near eighteen.' He asked her to bring him in and shortly she ushered in a well dressed boy of about ten or twelve years. Fearing that indeed he had been too hasty the previous day, he told her that he would immediately reverse his decision and release the boy from his sentence. He was unclear as to how the court record was to be amended to reflect his revised decision, but the head clerk, a grey haired man with many years of faithful service to a succession of DCs and ADCs, came to his rescue: 'Sir, I think you should simply alter the name of the accused in the record book and substitute the name of the next tax defaulter to appear before you whom you intend to convict. This is what your predecessors have done when this lady has come in with the same complaint. You see, Sir, she has two stable boys with the same name, the one you saw today, aged twelve, and the other you saw yesterday, aged twenty.'

Age was only one of the criteria of the liability to pay tax, for one also had to be able to pay or to secure the means of paying the tax. At a time when the Governor was pushing the production of cash crops for export, any African who could use a hoe could cultivate crops, sell them and thereby secure the means of paying his tax. Again the *boma* messengers were invaluable. They pointed out that a slightly darkened right thumb surface might suggest that the person's thumb had recently or regularly been applied to an inked pad and this was likely to indicate that their thumb print had been taken to validate vouchers when they received their pay. They would also invite the magistrate – the DC or ADC – to inspect the palms of the defaulter. If these were rough then it was evidence of manual labour in the gardens and consequently their owners were liable to pay tax, and were promptly convicted for failing to do so. On the other hand, if the palms were smooth, it was some evidence that the person concerned really was unwell, could not work and consequently was not liable to pay tax. None but the truly unwell male would risk the criticism and ridicule meted out in the village for the healthy who would not help to hoe the family garden.

The criterion for liability to pay tax that caused the least frequent problem was that of maleness: only males were subject to taxation. But, though rare, when it did crop up it was capable of causing the greatest difficulty. A District Commissioner's morning with paper work in the *boma* was interrupted by the sergeant messenger coming in to the office and saying 'We have a tax case here, Sah.' Glad of a break from the papers on his desk, the DC said, 'Bring him in and we will try him now.' The sergeant looked uncomfortable and said, 'Oh no, Sah, he's not a defaulter. He *wants* to pay his tax.' 'Well, then, why are you bothering me? Take him to the tax office and let him pay.' The sergeant respectfully but firmly said, 'I think you should see him, Sah.' A little irritated, the DC asked him to bring the man in. He did so: a shy, good-looking young man in his early twenties, dressed in white shirt, tie, black trousers and polished shoes, much smarter than the general run of tax defaulters. He was clearly over the age of eighteen and well able to work to pay his tax. The DC could not see what the problem was: either he was taken to the tax office and made to pay his tax or he tried him on the spot for tax default. 'We think you should see him, Sah.' 'But I can see him. He's standing in front of me. I'm not blind, dammit!' 'No, Sah, we think you should *see* him.' The DC was now both irritated and flummoxed. 'Take him outside, please, and then come back and tell me what this is all about.' He did so, and on his return - the DC having calmed down and the sergeant having worked out what he was to say - said, 'Sah, this man is not a man.' 'How the Devil can a man not be a man?' he demanded. 'Sah, this man is not a *man.*' The DC, fast loosing his grasp of what was going on and, more worrying, his grasp on sanity, told the sergeant that there was only one way to find out and he had better find out quickly. The sergeant, standing his ground, said he had already done so. Still puzzled, the DC asked if this was a woman dressed like a man, and was told, 'No, Sah, he – I mean she – is both a man and a woman. I still think you should *see* him - her.' This was getting them nowhere, so the DC said he would *see* the young person, but only if he agreed and in the presence of the sergeant and one of his fellow messengers. The young man readily agreed to a limited physical inspection. The sergeant discreetly closed the curtains of the office and invited the young man to drop his pants. This he politely did and after a very brief and none too close inspection, the DC concluded that the sergeant was correct when he said the young person was - externally, biologically - both man and woman. It transpired that he was anxious to be recognized as a male. Since all the medical men he had consulted had paid insufficient attention to the single lecture on hermaphroditic conditions at their medical schools, they had dithered inconclusively. Consequently, the young man was convinced that only the *boma* could confer this recognition. 'But how?' 'By letting me pay my tax because only men can pay tax.' The DC agreed. The young man pulled up his pants and went off happily to the tax office, his head held high, and paid his tax. A little later that morning he returned and asked if, as a great personal favour, the DC would personally countersign his tax receipt. The DC was pleased to oblige.

MESSENGER SERVICE

Semper aliquid novi ex Malawi.
Adapted from Pliny the Elder.

One of the informal and much appreciated services that *boma* messengers habitually rendered was that of drawing to their DC's and ADC's attention unusual things that they thought, usually correctly, might interest them. There are many examples. Julius was one and the hermaphrodite would-be tax payer was another.

There was, too, the villager who produced a primitive but totally effective instant glue long before the commercial world got round to anything like it. He arrived at the *boma* one day, accompanied by a messenger and followed by a band of small children, and was carrying a number of pieces of tree branch each about two feet long, and a further branch still bearing its leaves. He quietly chewed the leaves and with the saliva that this produced he stuck together the other branches to form a rough table. He held the pieces momentarily together, pressed them firmly and then stood back to admire his work and to invite the ADC to stand on the table. The ADC, with some reluctance, gingerly did so and the table showed not the slightest sign of collapsing even when he jumped up and down on it. It was as solid as a rock and remained so for several months until, running short of firewood in the kitchen, his cook tragically burned it and the secret was lost forever.

Moses was one of the most remarkable African musicians one could have ever met. He wore a shirt with so many unrepaired holes in it that one marvelled at his ability to take it off and put it on and to wash it. His khaki shorts, which ended somewhere between his knee and his ankle – one leg lower than the other – were in a better condition but only because the patches eventually outnumbered the areas of original cloth. In his hands he carried his 'guitar'. It was a contrivance consisting of sound boxes, made from a gourd and a biscuit tin, fixed to a two foot handle of wood at the end of which was a bicycle bell and along which was tightly stretched the strings, some of which were made of wire, some of cow hide and others of sisal. By strumming and plucking the strings, by tapping and beating the handle, by ringing the bicycle bell, by clapping his hands, by stamping his feet and by stroking the sound boxes, Moses accompanied himself as he sang impromptu songs of his own composition. It was a remarkable musical instrument and produced the most entertaining of sounds, but his singing was even more remarkable, for he covered the whole range of male voices from deep *basso profundo*, through rich baritone and lyric tenor, to counter tenor and falsetto. So far as is known and to the world's incomparable loss, Moses never performed in public and he did so in private only for his own enjoyment and, infrequently, for district officers and even then only if introduced by a *boma* messenger.

Finally, briefly, discreetly and reluctantly, there was the occasion when a *boma* messenger, with an ill concealed mixture of embarrassment and glee, suggested that the ADC might like to see a couple who were being carried to the local hospital on an ox cart by a group of their relatives accompanied by a police officer. It appears that the couple, married but regrettably not to each other, had been caught *in flagrante delicto* but had been so caught only because a curse had been placed on them by one or other of their lawful spouses and they had been unable to uncouple themselves, to disentangle themselves from what was to be their final copulative embrace. We do not know whether the ADC accepted the invitation. We do know that the hospital matron, sure that the gynaecologist would not wish to intervene, and muttering something about 'till death do us part', referred them to the veterinary surgeon; but we are unclear whether he was able to help.

ooo ☺ ☻ ooo

While watching a club game at Cholo
An excited young man shouted 'Goalo'.
The Captain said, 'come here,
I'd like a word in your ear.
We don't call them 'goals' when playing polo.'

ooo ☺ ☻ ooo

THE MAGOMERO CROSS

In 1959 a young Assistant District Commissioner was a lay member of the Anglican synod when it held its annual meeting. A state of emergency had recently been declared and this was a great worry to the church as it was to others. At the meeting the question of the centenary of the founding of the Universities Mission to Central Africa arose and a number of those present voiced the opinion that there could be no celebrations when so many people were imprisoned without trial during the emergency. Whilst sharing their general concern the ADC felt strongly that the centenary should be celebrated in Nyasaland and he said so, possibly too bluntly by pointing out that centenaries did not occur too often. This view, or more likely the way it had been expressed, was not well received. As the young man sat down, the

Attorney-General, also a member of synod, who was sitting next to him and who had played an important part in the declaration of the state of emergency, touched his arm and said, `You've torn it now. You'd better say something positive.' He stood up again and, without time to consider the possibilities of 'something positive', and saying as one does on such occasions the first thing that entered his head, suggested that the church make a pilgrimage to Magomero, the site of the first Christian mission station in the country. It was an off the cuff suggestion and dangerous because no one knew precisely where Magomero was. It so happened that he had been researching the question of the location of Magomero and was close, he thought, to being able to prove where it was - he subsequently published the evidence briefly in a geographical journal. Synod accepted his suggestion.

In readiness for the pilgrimage, a large metal cross was erected on the site of the original Magomero mission. A church-going member of the Public Works Department was asked if he could help with this. He found a few lengths of unwanted and a little rusty six inch steel water piping and agreed to make the cross. The length of the longest piece of the unwanted piping determined the height of the cross – some fourteen feet – and the design was drawn with a twig in the sand outside the Public Works Department office in Zomba by the church-going PWD official, the ADC and the Archdeacon of the Shire Highlands: a rare but splendid example of state-church cooperation.

The finished cross, painted in silver-grey, was set up - not without a certain amount of difficulty - within the Magomero site as close as could be determined to the point where the original mud and wattle church had been planned by Bishop MacKenzie and his colleagues in 1861. The ADC recalled thinking, as they dug the hole to erect the cross, how splendid it would be if they unearthed the sealed bottle which had been buried at the corner post when the church was started a hundred years previously and which contained papers giving details of the mission station and the church. In due course, the Archbishop of York came to Nyasaland and led a pilgrimage of huge numbers of church followers to the Magomero site, located within a rarely visited bend in the Namadzi river, and held an impressive service there.

Though it is unlikely, it is possible that the cross still stands today – six inch piping is rather large for making *kachasu* stills though it may have other uses. What is much more likely is that the ancient bottle with its historically precious papers still lies buried there. Maybe, the bicentenary of the UMCA in 2060 will be celebrated by another pilgrimage, this time accompanied by a working party of muscular Christian archaeologists searching for the bottle and its contents.

JANUARY 1 AND 2

In several countries of the world, children are given names that reflect the day or month of their birth. For example, in southern Ghana if one is born on a Sunday a male child is called Kwesi and a female is called Esi, and there are names for those born on every other day of the week: for a Saturday birth the boy becomes Kwame and the girl becomes Ama. In Britain, too, we have girls named April, May or June. And in Malawi one occasionally comes across a man called for example, January. I had the good fortune to know two of these.

JANUARY 1

The first of my Januaries was a *boma* sergeant messenger. He had served in the KAR during the Second World War and had joined the *boma* staff on demobilization in 1946. He was a much decorated soldier and was deeply respected as a man who got things done, though no one at that time, thankfully, would have used the term 'task oriented'. Although he was not a particularly tall person, he had a commanding presence and this - with the impressively loud voice, developed over many years on parade grounds in various parts of the world, with which he issued instructions to the other messengers, labourers and carriers – helped to account for his reputation as a disciplined and efficient leader of men.

At no time did this reputation display itself better than when accompanying the District Commissioner on *ulendo*. Just before first light each morning Sergeant January could be heard cursing the idle labourers accompanying the DC and ordering them to raise their lazy bodies from their sleeping mats and get a move on, sweep the surrounds and get the loads packed ready to start off later in the morning for their next destination. He then turned his attention to his fellow messengers, alternately criticizing and praising their turnout, commenting on the polishing of their boots and leather belts, the starching and ironing of their uniforms, the angle of their fezzes and the shine of their brass cap badges and buttons. All this was conducted *sotto voce* in a well practised stage whisper, that is, whilst pretending not to be heard by the DC, who was still slumbering, was loud enough to ensure that he clearly understood that the sergeant was up and about and living up to his well deserved reputation for discipline and efficiency. Then, at the moment the sergeant judged that the DC was about to rise, have his early morning tea, shave and dress, January gradually turned up the volume of his instructions, paraded the messengers and marched them up and down the area just outside the DC's tent. Finally, as the DC emerged from his tent,

Sergeant January roared his messengers to attention, slammed his boots and gave an impressive salute: 'Moni, Sah!'

January was always profoundly gratified to see the friendly and admiring smile on the DC's face as he returned the salute. What he did not know, and no one ever had the unkindness to tell him – not even the messengers, carriers and labourers accompanying him – was that the DC and his predecessors had for years derived much private pleasure in delaying their appearance each morning when on *ulendo* in order to give Sergeant January time fully to get everything in spick and span order. More importantly, they did so because it gave them time to observe, through one of the many small holes in the canvas walls of the tent, the way in which all of it was conducted from January's sleeping mat. He gave all his instructions, did all his checking and drilling, shaved and dressed himself without once rising from the mat. Only at the very last moment did he rise, roll up his mat and blanket and place them on one side, ready to salute the District Commissioner.

JANUARY 2

The second of my Januaries was a very different sort of person. He was one of the most handsome men I have met. He was tall, erect and well built, his eyes sparkled in his black shining face, his teeth were even and the whitest imaginable, his jet black curly beard and hair were rather longer than those of many men of similar age – he was, I guess, about forty when I first met him. He lived on the outskirts of Limbe into which sprawling township he would walk with his sturdy wheelbarrow each morning to conduct his business.

And what was that business? Well, he was a practitioner of re-cycling, though the term was not then current, and he could not bear to see good rejected materials go to waste. On his daily forays he would devote many hours to scouring the rear quarters of the Asian trading stores, collecting disused cardboard boxes, tins, jars, bottles and newspapers. Save for the glass jars and bottles – for these were the days before plastic containers were used – he would carefully press his collected materials flat and place them all on his wheelbarrow, a vehicle that he had made himself and which some folk saw as having wheels that were not quite round, while less charitable observers saw them as being not quite square. Late each afternoon, January would return, usually quite heavily laden, to his house. Here he would place the things he had so assiduously collected, neatly inside the house, carefully climb in and go to sleep on top of his accumulated gatherings, ready for an early start the next day. When his house, with its simple reed walls and grass roof, became so full that he could no longer find room to sleep, he built himself a new house next to it, and started all over again. In the course of time he came to have a whole string of houses, neatly spaced in a straight line along the road side.

Eventually, the town planning bureaucrats felt that enough was enough; that January's houses, and particularly their contents, were an unsightly blot on the township's edge. The planning laws would have to be enforced and the houses, together with their contents, would have to be destroyed.

Just after he was told what was about to happen, January varied his daily routine to call on the District Commissioner, who was surprised to see him, for although like many people he had observed his growing line of houses, he had never spoken with him, nor indeed did he know anyone else who had heard him utter a word. He was further astonished when January addressed him in near perfect, well modulated, English and spoke of the threat to his dwellings.

Though not sanguine of success, the DC said he would see what he could do. He spent several hours pouring over and carefully studying the relevant legislation and maps and making detailed notes. The following morning he asked the Senior Town Planning Officer to call on him. When he arrived, the DC pointed out that although there existed a number of apparent inconsistencies and a lack of clarity in the legislation, the essential fact was that the place where January lived was a few feet outside the township boundary and his houses were therefore beyond the remit and bureaucratic clutches of the town planners. Disappointed, the Senior Town Planning Officer agreed.

Late that afternoon the DC went to see January and found him quietly unpacking his neatly folded newspapers and cardboard boxes from his wheelbarrow outside the latest of his houses. As he began to explain the good news to him, January politely held up his hand, went into one of the earliest of his houses, and emerged with a large envelope which he placed on the ground next to him. He indicated to the DC that he should carry on with what he was saying. When the DC had finished explaining the law and the outcome of his researches and his discussions with the Senior Town Planning Officer, January smiled and said, 'I know.' He then pulled from the envelope at his feet a well thumbed and carefully annotated copy of the Town Planning Ordinance together with a copy of the township map on which he had drawn the township boundary in red pencil and the location of his houses in blue pencil. 'You see, I found these papers behind the town council offices several years ago when I first came to live here and had to decide precisely where to settle. I was sure they would come in handy one day.'

NEAR MISSES

I am escaped with the skin of my teeth.
Job 19:20.

I

When he was arrested on 3 March 1959, Dr. Banda was taken in a Police Land Rover from his home in Limbe to Chileka from where he was flown to Southern Rhodesia to be detained in Gwelo Gaol. His arrest was effected just before daylight, and as the Land Rover was being driven speedily down the hill from Nyambadwe towards the airport, the driver saw a vehicle approaching him with its headlights dimmed. He moved over a little to pass the vehicle and only at the very last moment did he realize that it was not, as he had supposed judging by the space between the headlights, a car or small lorry but a large military armoured vehicle whose headlights were located close together and a yard or more from its sides. Had the Land Rover driver, a former Metropolitan Police flying squad officer, not swerved very sharply indeed to the soft shoulder of the road, his vehicle and its occupants would have crashed almost head-on with the armoured vehicle - and history would have been very different.

II

After his release from detention in April 1960, Dr. Banda visited the United States and was booked into a hotel in New York. Great consternation was caused when, as he registered at reception, it was noticed for the first time that one of the other guests who had just booked in was Sir Roy Welensky, the Federal prime minister, the Doctor's political arch enemy and the man to whom his arrest and detention was widely attributed. Deft diplomatic choreography, with the help of well remunerated bell boys, ensured that neither of the two crossed the other's path. Dr. Banda was not made aware of the problem but had he been he would surely have wondered if he would ever be rid of Sir Roy.

III

Towards the end of 1963, just a few days before the Federation of Rhodesia and Nyasaland was finally abolished, the Governor-General, Lord Dalhousie, paid his last official visit to Nyasaland and stayed with the Governor at Government House in Zomba. Given the political sensitivities over all things federal, the exuberance of the Malawians with the Federation's abolition and the imminence of self-government, little publicity was given to the Governor-General's visit. It was felt proper, however, that when he left Zomba to travel via Blantyre - where, after a short courtesy call on the Mayor - he would travel on to Chileka airport, he should be given a police motor cycle escort and that his car should fly the Federal flag. He was scheduled to leave Zomba at ten o'clock in the morning.

Shortly after 8.00 a.m. the Private Secretary to the Governor learned that at precisely the same time as Lord Dalhousie was due to leave Zomba for Blantyre, Dr. Banda was to leave Blantyre for Zomba on his way to a huge rally at Domasi. The Doctor habitually travelled in a large and fast moving cavalcade with Malawi Congress Party escorts of Land Rovers packed with white uniformed members of his bodyguard and with sirens blaring to warn other road users that they should immediately get out of the way. There had been a disturbing number of incidents in which members of the public had not moved quickly enough and had been forced off the road, thrown into the ditches beside the highway and seriously assaulted.

With terrifying visions of the Governor-General's sedate black car, flying its official flag and accompanied by blue uniformed police motorcyclists meeting, half way between Blantyre and Zomba, the fast moving, siren blaring, MCP red beflagged vehicles of the Doctor's cavalcade with its white uniformed, cock-a-hoop guards, the Private Secretary set about engineering a quick solution. He persuaded the Governor to take his time over their breakfast of kedgeree, devilled kidneys, kippers, eggs, bacon, toast and marmalade and coffee – and yet more coffee - and engage the Governor-General in unusually lengthy pleasantries and anecdotes. He also telephoned to Blantyre and told the Mayor that the Governor-General was unfortunately taking so long over his breakfast that they were running late and would have to go straight to Chileka and not be able to stop off at Blantyre.

Eventually, by leaving late and cutting out the Blantyre visit, the Governor-General's party left Government House only seconds after Dr. Banda's cavalcade passed through Zomba. Neither the Doctor, excited by the prospects of a successful political meeting at Domasi and his imminent appointment as the country's first prime minister, nor the Governor-General, about to lose his job but delightfully replete with a splendid breakfast, learned that they had so closely missed a potentially catastrophic confrontation on the highway.

IV

The legal instrument granting independence to former African colonies was an Act of the British Parliament, but its provisions were brought into effect, made operative, by an Order in Council. The day before the Duke of Edinburgh was due to fly out to Malawi to represent the Queen at the Independence Day celebrations, it was discovered by an Under Secretary at the Commonwealth Relations Office that the necessary Order in Council had not been signed by the Queen. He immediately told the Permanent Secretary. 'Well', said the Permanent Secretary calmly, 'Kindly get Her Majesty to sign it.' 'But', replied the civil servant he was addressing, 'she's in Scotland, at Balmoral.' 'Ah', said the Permanent Secretary, long skilled in the art of turning mountains into molehills, 'then I believe you must quickly fly up to Scotland, drive to Balmoral and get Her Majesty to sign it.' 'But it is an Order in Council and the signing of it requires the presence of at least three Privy Councillors.' 'My dear fellow, find three Privy Counsellors – there are dozens of them about these days – and take them with you to Scotland.' And so it was. The signed Order in Council arrived back in London just in time for it to be handed to the Prince's equerry on the aircraft steps as they boarded the VC10 of the Queen's Flight to take them to Malawi.

ooo ☺ ☻ ooo

FAMOUS LAST WORDS

'You need have no fears. You will be able to complete a full career in the Colonial Service in Africa, and so, I am confident, will your son.' Colonial Office official interviewing a candidate for the Colonial Service, 1956. The following year the Gold Coast became independent and within a decade all other British colonies in Africa followed suit.

'The British Government has no intention of abolishing the Federation. It is here to stay.' Alan Lennox Boyd, Colonial Secretary, 1958, repeating a similar statement made by the Foreign Secretary, slightly earlier. Five years later the British Government abolished the Federation.

'No, I have not been asked to join the Monckton Commission, and if I am asked I intend to decline.' Elspeth Huxley, November 1959. The list of members of the Commission, announced less than a month later, to advise on the future of the Federation, included Mrs. Huxley's name.

At a press conference in Zomba on 2 March 1959, the Governor, Sir Robert Armitage, was asked if he needed to declare a state of emergency before using military force if the police could not handle the situation. He replied. 'Not necessarily.' When asked if the ordinary law enabled the Government to proscribe Congress without resort to declaring a state of emergency, he replied, 'Yes.' At midnight that day he declared a state of emergency and proscribed Congress.

'On grounds of principle I will not leave the country. This would be an act of desertion or betrayal of our supporters by me.' Henry Chipembere, 7 March 1965. On 27 April 1965, Chipembere flew from Malawi into voluntary and permanent exile in the USA.

'The unity of the country is beyond challenge', Sir Henry Phillips; 'Dr. Banda has achieved a remarkable degree of unity throughout the nation. There is no question of any threat to the unity of the Malawi Congress Party', Sir Bryan Roberts; 'The degree to which Malawi has achieved national unity has few parallels in Africa. Malawians are remarkably of one mind', Clyde Sanger; 'The country is united as never before', Colin Cameron. All on the eve of Malawi's independence. Two months later a cabinet crisis removed all but one of the ministers and split the country into deep and lasting factions.

'There may be localized food shortages but there is no famine', Christopher Garnett, the Director of Agriculture, 1948. Within days, feeding camps had to be opened and hundreds of tons of maize had to be imported to save starving villagers.

'This is not a cabinet crisis', Dr. Banda, 9 September 1964, seven of his nine cabinet ministers having resigned or been dismissed, never to return.

'I have spoken with the Prime Minister and he assures me that you will be quite safe in visiting him at his house.' Sir Glyn Jones to Orton Chirwa, September 1964. An hour later Chirwa returned from the Doctor's house, having been viciously attacked and seriously injured by the Prime Minister's bodyguard.

'Why are those men waving at us?' A Peace Corps Volunteer to her companion who had driven onto the main Blantyre-Zomba road from a side road and found himself in the centre of the President's cavalcade, wedged between the President's red Mercedes and the green Land Rovers filled with furiously gesticulating, white uniformed, members of his bodyguard.

ooo ☺ ☻ ooo

A MARK OF DISTINCTION

Malawi anecdotes have the unique and outstanding distinction that one of their number has been recounted publicly from the pulpit at a service in St. Paul's Cathedral in London. No other African anecdote has been honoured in this way, and it is most unlikely that any will be in the future. Furthermore, and bestowing additional distinction, it was related by a member of the House of Lords, a peer of the realm, no less a worthy than Lord Ackner, a most distinguished jurist and a Lord of Appeal in Ordinary. Lord Ackner, following the discipline of his profession in always citing the authorities on which he was depending, generously - and embarrassingly - acknowledged the authorship of the anecdote.

The anecdote in question shows the excellent relations between Dr. Banda and Sir Bryan Roberts, Secretary to the President and Cabinet. It also shows an aspect of Dr. Banda's humour. He had spent significantly more years living in Western countries, America and Britain, than had Sir Bryan who had joined the Colonial Legal Service as a young man. Dr. Banda had left his homeland in his early teens and had not returned until he was about sixty, and he knew English colloquial expressions every bit as well as did his Cabinet Secretary. It was a little joke between the two of them that the Doctor should pretend otherwise.

The occasion was the memorial service for Sir Bryan Roberts. Lord Ackner was to deliver the eulogy and he sought advice on anecdotes about Sir Bryan. There was no difficulty in recalling anecdotes, because he was a rich source of amusing stories. The difficulty was that whilst amusing, in some cases hilariously side-splitting, the stories were not the sort that could be told in a place of worship where the uncontrollable giggling, guffawing and thigh slapping that they might engender would be unseemly, and where the inclusion of the names of others involved might immediately result in the issue of a writ of defamation. These were risks that a Law Lord could not for one moment countenance.

After much head scratching and unsuccessfully considering the possibilities that some might not be sailing too close to the edges of propriety, one anecdote seemed to the person he consulted to be just acceptable and it was suggested, with a good deal of trepidation, to Lord Ackner. The noble Law Lord expressed his gratitude and felt, as did the person suggesting it, that whilst not a good anecdote, it was the best – indeed the only one – available. The story he related, thereby bringing such distinction upon Malawi anecdotage, was this:

At a cabinet meeting when a matter concerning the regulation of the legal profession was being discussed, Dr. Banda remarked, 'Gentlemen, it is well known that all lawyers are liars.' He leaned forward, turned to Sir Bryan, nodded politely and added, 'Present company excepted, of course. Remind me, please, Sir Bryan, isn't that the expression you use in England? Yes, present company excepted. As I was saying, gentlemen, all lawyers are liars.'

MANGOES ON THE MOON: MALAWI FLAVOURED LIMERICKS

The notion of expressing sentiments in short lines having similar sounds at their ends seems as remote as mangoes on the moon.
Philip Larkin.

Initially, all the limericks in this anthology were collected and placed - gathered and planted, as it were – together in this chapter, but some, like other mangoes which spread and seem to grow everywhere, filling spare gaps where they can find them, have broken loose and are now found distributed in various places throughout the volume. Others, however, have been better behaved and have stayed where they were originally placed – here:

A store-keeper I knew in Mchinji
was uncommonly mean and quite stingy.
Though far from being poor,
his house had no door
and inside was distressingly dingy.

A pharmacist who worked in Fort Hill
invented a marvellous new pill.
It cured one of the pox
but rotted one's socks
and his return on his investment was nil.

A student who lived at Nkotakota
drove home in a fanciful motor.
But what caused his friends
to double up with the bends
was his Kamuzu Academy straw boater.

An equestrian fellow from Chongoni
boasted he always rode on a pony.
But for all his talk
he continued to walk
and everyone thought he was looney.

NYASALAND-MALAWI ANECDOTES

A traditional dancer from Madziabango
was converted to the Argentine tango.
This brought him much strife
especially as his wife
infinitely preferred the fandango.

In my youth by the lake at Chipoka
I met a young lady, a good-looker.
When I went back this year,
I shed a sad tear,
to learn that she'd gone: *wachoka*.

A musician from the Conservatoire Mwanza
wrote an oratorio, stanza by stanza.
But the extraordinary thing
was his ability to sing
in the style of Mario Lanza.

Do you remember the Copper from Tuchila
who arrested a notorious stealer?
Awarded the QPM,
He said, 'It's a gem
But I'm only an old fashioned Peeler.'

A prospector, the son of Lord Canning,
was found in a stream near Fort Manning.
He was looking for gold,
or so I was told,
and when I saw him he certainly was panning.

I recall a young man from Mpemba
who was born, if I rightly remember,
on the eve of the seventh
or was it the eleventh?
In any case the month was Jufember.

The internet café at Lake Chiuta
was the haunt of an ardent young suitor.
He made date after date
and sealed many a fate
with just a tap on his home made computer.

NYASALAND-MALAWI ANECDOTES

Hurtling down the road to Chileka
in his *galimoto,* an ancient bone-shaker,
he passed a police patrol,
fully out of control
and ended up in the arms of his Maker

A reckless employer from Ncheu
said to his staff, 'What say you?
I've been very rash
and now have no cash
and thus I no longer can pay you.'

Some Peace Corps volunteers in Malawi
got lost in the bush near Bandawe.
They were found the next day,
I'm happy to say,
by shouting out 'Where the hell are we?'

A school leaver I know, name of Stella,
got work in a bank as a teller,
though not in the city
which she thought was a pity
but out in the bush at Mponela

In the office one day with H.E.
he frowned and then said to me,
'Pass the draft honours list
So I can see who I've missed
And then we can break for some tea.'

A close friend and his wife, my dear sister,
lived idyllically on the slopes of Fort Lister.
When e'er she went away
if only for a day
he wept and most dreadfully missed her.

Lived a man near the Mozambique border
with Obsessive Limerick Disorder.
A skilled psychiatric nurse
could have helped with this curse
but, alas, the poor chap can't afford her.

GLOSSARY

achimwene, my friend
ADC Assistant District Commissioner
A de C Aide de Camp
askari soldier
bastinado stick used for corporal punishment
boma government station; District Commissioner's office
bwana master; Sir
capitao foreman
chakudya food
chimbuzi latrine; lavatory
CS Chief Secretary
DC District Commissioner
debe bucket, often old paraffin tin
dona lady; Madam
fodya tobacco
galimoto motor car
GH Government House
HE His Excellency; the Governor
Inde, Indithu yes; yes indeed
kachasu traditionally distilled liquor
kale long ago
khonde verandah
machila hammock for carrying people
maso eyes
mbawa mahogany
moa beer
msanga msanga quickly
mtedza groundnuts
muli bwanji? how are you?
njobvu elephant
nkhokwe granary
nthawi time
nyama meat
odi 'hello' when about to enter a house
palmatoria wooden paddle used for corporal punishment
patali far
PC Provincial Commissioner
posho ration money or food
supuliya aluminium saucepan
ulendo journey
UMCA Universities Mission to Central Africa
wachoka cleared off